Reasonable Use of Force
by Police

STUDIES IN CRIME & PUNISHMENT

David A. Schultz and Christina DeJong
General Editors

Vol. 17

PETER LANG
New York • Washington, D.C./Baltimore • Bern
Frankfurt am Main • Berlin • Brussels • Vienna • Oxford

David A. May & James E. Headley

Reasonable Use of Force by Police

Seizures, Firearms, and High-Speed Chases

l60201

PETER LANG

New York • Washington, D.C./Baltimore • Bern

Frankfurt am Main • Berlin • Brussels • Vienna • Oxford

Library of Congress Cataloging-in-Publication Data

May, David A.
Reasonable use of force by police: seizures, firearms,
and high-speed chases / David A. May, James E. Headley.
p. cm. — (Studies in crime and punishment; v. 17)
Includes bibliographical references.
1. Police training. 2. Police—Equipment and supplies.
3. Restraint of prisoners. 4. Self-defense for police.
5. Firearms—Use in crime prevention.
6. Police pursuit driving. I. Title.
HV7923.M39   363.2'32—dc22   2008002913
ISBN 978-0-8204-6934-8
ISSN 1529-2444

Bibliographic information published by **Die Deutsche Bibliothek.**
Die Deutsche Bibliothek lists this publication in the "Deutsche
Nationalbibliografie"; detailed bibliographic data is available
on the Internet at http://dnb.ddb.de/.

Cover design by Clear Point Designs

The paper in this book meets the guidelines for permanence and durability
of the Committee on Production Guidelines for Book Longevity
of the Council of Library Resources.

Printed in the United States of America

Contents

Introduction: Understanding Use of Force   **1**

The Necessity of Force   3

Checks on Force   8

Questions for Discussion   11

1. Seizure, Searches, Probable Cause, and Arrest   **13**

The Fourth Amendment Standards   14

The Exclusionary Rule   16

Probable Cause and Arrest   27

Privacy Expectations and Constitutional Law   34

Ethics and Discretion   39

Questions for Discussion   40

2. Use of Lethal and Nonlethal Force   **43**

Proportionality and Physical Force   44

Use of Lethal Force   46

Less Lethal Alternatives   54

Crowd Control and Siege Situations   59

Operation Order   61

Case Study: Ruby Ridge—What Went Wrong?   62

Case Study: World Series Crowd
    Control—What Went Wrong?   65
Importance of Training/Certification   65
Documenting Use of Force   66
Hypotheticals   66
Questions for Discussion   67

3. Custodial Interrogation   **69**
What Is Custodial Interrogation?   69
Due Process   75
Costs and Benefits   77
Pretext Stops and Traffic Stops
    as Custodial Interrogation   85
Questions for Discussion   91

4. Liability of Law Enforcement Officers   **93**
Civil Liability   94
Criminal Liability   105
Rampart   106
Questions for Discussion   109

5. High-Speed Pursuit   **111**
Introduction—*Scott v. Harris*   111
Definition of Pursuit and Scope of the Question   113
Cases   116
Policy and Training   121
Questions for Discussion   124

Conclusion: Reasonable Use of Force by Police   **125**

Glossary of Key Definitions   **131**

Key Cases and Holdings   **137**

Notes   **143**

Introduction: Understanding Use of Force

The use of force by police is the most serious decision and one of the most significant interactions law enforcement officers can have with citizens. The decisions made by political and administrative officials when they determine matters of policy[1] or the decisions made by individual officers in split seconds may be decisions of life and death importance. So, it stands to reason that the determination of proper use of force by law enforcement at both administrative and individual levels is crucial for both law enforcement and for the public to maintain order, protect society, enforce just laws, and reasonably respect and protect the rights of civilian citizens.

Those decisions however are seldom easy to make. Consider, as examples, the decisions to use appropriate force in the following three examples. Each scenario is a real example of law enforcement's use of physical force in serious and difficult situations and each presents different challenges to the officers involved.

Scenario 1[2]

Deputy Beaumont and Deputy Robert Inn responded to a domestic violence call in King County, Washington. They were responding to a woman's report that her boyfriend was distraught and armed with a knife. When the law enforcement officers arrived on the scene, everyone in the home was armed: the boyfriend who had been the subject of the original call was wielding a steak knife, Deputy Beaumont held his Glock semiautomatic handgun and Deputy Inn had drawn his M-26 Taser. The officers observed a dangerous situation. "As they approached, the boyfriend, blood smeared on his face from a cut on his wrist, suddenly leaped from the couch where he'd been sitting and lunged at them. The man was well within the 21-foot safety zone that an officer in that jurisdiction learns in training is the minimum distance needed to draw a weapon and shoot an armed assailant." To end the situation and the threats posed by it, Deputy Inn fired the Taser and the suspect was subdued and arrested.

Did police use reasonable force to apprehend the suspect? Could or should the police have used more, even deadly force against the suspect? Should the police have attempted to employ less force to achieve the objective? What is a reasonable amount of force for police to have used in this or in a similar situation?

Scenario 2[3]

The incident began on a Saturday evening when a city police officer stopped four people on Cincinnati Street between Baldwin and Ermina avenues after reports that someone had stolen Keystone Ice beer from the Maid O'Clover convenience store. The officer ordered all four individuals to sit on the curb. Three of the men said that they complied, but that one boy, Eagle Michael, had not. Other witnesses at the scene and at the time said to the officer that the boy, Michael, had a gun. The officer retreated, according to the police account of the incident, trying to keep the patrol car between herself and the suspect, Michael. "Don't shoot, it's a BB gun," the three men on the curb reportedly told the officer. The officer repeatedly yelled an order to Michael, "put the gun down, put the gun down." As Michael bent down to pick up the beer, the officer yelled at him again to put the gun down, and then she fired. The 15-year-old, Eagle Michael, was killed. It turned out that he did have a BB gun, and that he also had a hearing problem. A witness to the shooting said, "If it was a BB gun … it sure looked like a 9 mm or a .45. It was a big gun."

The shooting of Eagle Michael was certainly tragic. But was the shooting an unreasonable use of force by police? What other steps could or should the officer reasonably have taken? Or did the officer act properly?

Scenario 3[4]

Siege situations are unusual, and everyone in law enforcement seeks to avoid them if at all possible; still siege situations do occur and should be considered when examining use of force by law enforcement. The incident at Ruby Ridge stands out as an anomaly in officers' use of force for federal law enforcement. Ruby Ridge involved a massive siege situation in which there was a standoff between agents of the ATF, FBI, as well as other federal and state agencies, and Randy Weaver and his family and Kevin Harris barricaded in a cabin in North Idaho beginning in August of 1992. The siege ultimately lasted about eleven days. This infamous incident, from which law enforcement learned much, is discussed in more detail in Chapter Two of this book.[5] While there remain to this day many questions surrounding what happened at Ruby Ridge, FBI sharpshooter, Lon Horiuchi, did receive "modified" rules of engagement. Those modifications told him that adults who were barricaded in the cabin could and should be neutralized. After receiving those modified rules, Lon Horiuchi aimed and fired his powerful sniper's rifle. Vicki Weaver, one of the occupants of the cabin in the siege, was struck and killed by the FBI sharpshooter's bullet.

What rules of engagement did Agent Horiuchi employ? Did the sharpshooter use deadly force reasonably and lawfully? Should Horiuchi have exercised his own judgment differently and refrained from firing the shot that killed Vickie Weaver? What rule regarding use of lethal force should Horiuchi have employed in the siege situation? What rule governs use of lethal force by law enforcement officers?

The Necessity of Force

This book will examine questions about police use of force such as those raised in these three scenarios. It is not easy to arrive at the answers and seldom do all members of the communities affected agree with the answers. One proposition, to which all should agree, however, is the necessity of some level of force in the hands of police is an essential part of the policing function.("As long as members of society do not comply with law and resist the police, force will remain an inevitable part of policing."[6])

It might be possible to decide in some objective fashion whether the modifications to the rules of engagement relied upon by Horiuchi were authentic and whether they were properly issued on the basis of the FBI's bureaucratic procedures. It might not be too difficult to determine whether the officer who shot Eagle Michael had followed her department's guidelines on use of force and had followed them correctly. Those questions, however, are only one part of the equation in use of force and the decisions that must be made about individual actions as well as broader questions of law and policy. Because police use of force, and police use of explicitly deadly force in particular, can have tremendous consequences, other factors including political and ethical factors have to be considered as well. The consequences of police use of force have real and significant impact not only on the objects of that force, but also on the officers who employ the force, the agencies within which those officers work, and the communities in which they work and serve.

This book is intended for use in police training, police departments, universities, and by anyone interested in understanding the standards of reasonable use of force by police and other law enforcement officers. At a minimum, all law enforcement officers must understand and internalize the standards, laws, rules, and policies connected with their use of force. They must do so to a degree that will allow them to employ those standards in their everyday working lives regularly, efficiently, correctly, and safely. Thus, law enforcement officers need to know not only how much and what kind of force they should or are allowed to use in particular situations but must also understand the moral, ethical, and legal consequences of using that force.

Many other actors in the criminal justice, legal, and political science fields need to understand reasonable use of force for a variety of reasons. Police officers need useable guidelines governing the reasonable use of force. Lawyers, prosecutors, and defense attorneys among others, need to know the legal limits of police use of force. Political scientists who study police use of force need to understand both how society governs itself and uses its monopoly on legitimate force in ways that are politically, economically, and morally justifiable. Responsible and informed citizens must be educated on what constitutes reasonable use of force by police in various situations and circumstances to be able to evaluate the actions of individual officers or entire departments and to be able to participate in the process of defining the rules in an informed manner.

Police and other law enforcement officers must sometimes make rapid, even split-second decisions regarding the use of force as in the three scenarios described above. And, while those decisions must often be made very rapidly, the results of those decisions can be very real, very serious, or even tragic and have long-term repercussions. Many of the decisions made will ultimately be evaluated and reevaluated by many other actors with significantly more time to make those evaluations than the officer had to make her initial determination. Given also that those split-second decisions are often based on incomplete or imperfect information, it is possible to see why questions surrounding police use of force are often misunderstood by the general public and even by those in positions of authority who review officer decisions or even those involved in policymaking.

As we examine issues regarding police use of force, it is important to remember that there are two levels to the questions surrounding use of force questions; there is the theory of police use of force and there is reality. The reasonableness of use of force depends in part upon the circumstances that the officer is in at the time, his or her perceptions of that reality, and the information, or lack of it, available at the moment a decision has to be made. The law is clear, as the Supreme Court explicitly set out a test for when the use of deadly force is appropriate in the case of *Tennessee v. Garner,* which is discussed in detail in Chapter Two. Regarding the use of nondeadly or less lethal, force, the Supreme Court set out a test in the case of *Graham v. Connor* and it is explored in more detail in Chapter Two and Chapter Four. Please also see our proposed Use of Force Continuum in Chapter Two for guidance on the situational use of force. It is relatively easy as academics to outline in a book such as this the bright-line rules that exist in the law, the pronouncements of the Supreme Court in its opinions, or in the regulations of various law enforcement agencies. In practice, on the street, those bright lines may quickly become blurred for an officer by the pace of the real life events confronting her.

When people think of use of force by police, they might typically think of police using firearms to shoot suspects. That is one obvious example of police use of force and undoubtedly an important, serious, and often sensationalized application of police force, and one that frequently receives the most attention in the media. However, it may not be the most important use of force in the minds of police and other law enforcement officials as they do their jobs. Law enforcement officers necessarily use a much wider variety of types of force and in a wide variety of circumstances. From a show of authority with the flashing lights of the patrol car to make a traffic stop, to the physical presence of a uniformed officer, to putting handcuffs on a suspect, to using a Taser to apprehend a dangerous suspect, to outright use of the most deadly forms of force to apprehend a person who is an imminent danger to others, law enforcement officers must quickly choose from a wide range of types of possible force and then employ their choice properly.

KEY DEFINITION 1—USE OF FORCE (BY POLICE)

> Use of Force by police is any expression of force that is meant to produce specific law-enforcement-related results. These expressions can include physical, uniformed police presence (at the minimal end of the continuum on use of force), flashing patrol car lights, foot or vehicle pursuit, use of fists and holds, batons, aerosols, Tasers, less lethal projectiles, water cannons, and firearms (at the maximum end of the continuum on use of force).

How police determine how much force to use in these various circumstances and others is the subject of this book. There is no question that police must use some level of force in many situations, but society demands that the application of force must be carefully controlled, that law enforcement must use the right amount of force for the situation, no more and no less. In short, the needs of law enforcement to do the job that society gives it, must be balanced against the other needs of the society in which it operates.

Too little force applied in a situation may result in a subject or suspect getting away; and allowing that may be putting the officers and society at risk immediately or in the future, an outcome that most find unacceptable. With the application of too much or incorrect force, the suspect may be unnecessarily injured or killed and others including innocent civilians or other bystanders may also be injured or killed. When such tragic incidents occur, they may outrage the community, create a more difficult law enforcement environment, lead to protest and demonstrations, or result in civil lawsuits, or even criminal charges against the law enforcement officers involved. Most individuals recognize the need for law enforcement and the necessity of the use of a wide range of types of force. It is the balance between that need and others that can and does create an often uncomfortable tension.

To help law enforcement strike the proper balance in the use of force, new less lethal technologies are increasingly available for use in situations in which police try to apprehend an unwilling suspect. Legally, as well as ethically and morally, police have a responsibility to establish guidelines for the use of these new technologies, and police have a duty to use less lethal means to apprehend suspects when feasible and reasonable. Less lethal weapons such as Tasers should allow police the possibility of subduing even a violent suspect with an electronic jolt, rather than by using traditional firearms to shoot and possibly kill the suspect. Various types of rubber bullets and bean bag projectiles, rather than real bullets, are increasingly available. Other older, less lethal means are available as well. Implements and devices such as water cannons, tear gas, and pepper spray may provide officers with a wide range of options in the application of force as the situation warrants. And yes, the old standby, the application of personal physical force, is still available to the officer.

The reader should notice that we use the phrase "less lethal" when discussing these specific means of applying force. Certainly almost any application of force can be lethal in some situations, and everyone in law enforcement needs to be aware of that reality. So, while options for police use of force range from less lethal types to more lethal types with physical force being at the less lethal end of the continuum and the use of firearms and high-speed police chases being at the more lethal use of force end of the continuum, officers must choose carefully what type of force to apply and how to apply that force. Those decisions are constrained by the theory of use of force and the explicit standards of the agency for which they work and the broader rules established in applicable federal or state law.

One aspect of the use of force that is discussed first may seem less clear cut than the others. Police use of force usually relies on some type of seizure. Seizures usually come before searches. The other is the question of search and seizure with searches dependent upon the underlying seizure. Neither is probably what most would think of when confronted with the phrase "use of force." However, examination reveals that nearly all uses of force do in fact involve a seizure under the law. For example, police shooting a suspect dead is actually a seizure of the suspect. While both search and seizure are, in some senses, an application of force by an officer, searches typically depend upon seizures as the primary use of force. The Fourth Amendment recognizes as do most books on the subject including this one that seizure and search go hand in hand. However, while the primary goal of an officer is often a search for evidence, a seizure must come first. Most usually a person, car, house, or other thing is seized, and then subsequently searched. Practically and legally in many cases, the issues of seizure and search are inseparable. Like the bulbs in a line of Christmas tree lights, each bulb or each part of the case (search or seizure) must check out properly for the whole line of lights, or for the whole case, to work properly. So, while this book focuses on issues surrounding seizure as use of force it also, of necessity, discusses some related aspects of the law regarding searches. A successful use of force accomplishes an actual seizure within the meaning of the Fourth Amendment, and therefore seizures are examined as Fourth Amendment issues in this book.

Checks on Force

The issue of the use of force by law enforcement often becomes synonymous in the minds of many with the idea of excessive use of force.[7]

As has already been stated, the proper use of force is an essential role for law enforcement and this book focuses on the use of force by police in particular situations. There are many checks against unreasonable police use of force both internal and external. The morals, ethics, and judgment of individual law enforcement officers coupled with department morals, ethics, and culture, augmented and reinforced by both initial and continued training, and backstopped by internal affairs investigations, all act as internal checks on law enforcement in its application of force. External constraints include external investigations and audits, media investigations and the stories that result, public pressure, lawsuits, and even criminal prosecutions. Elements of all these checks against unreasonable use of force by police are covered to some extent in this book, but because reasonable use of force is far more important than the few instances of excessive or unreasonable force,[8] the primary focus of this book is on establishing and explaining coherent sets of guidelines for the reasonable use of force by police.[9]

It is functionally very difficult if not impossible to establish clear, immutable, bright line, or black and white rules on the reasonable use of force by police that are practically applicable in every circumstance, as a particular incident may be very fluid and fast moving. In addition, individual jurisdictions and agencies use different definitions, criteria, and standards and make cross-comparisons or simple statements nearly impossible.[10] The use of force by law enforcement is situational and the use and application of force often depend upon the circumstances of the particular incident that may be very fluid and fast moving. That reality makes it difficult to create bright line rules that hold true for every exercise of force that may be necessary. It is possible however to establish general guidelines for the reasonable use of force by police, guidelines that can then be interpreted and applied by individuals in the particular circumstances in which they are needed. After careful examination of specific examples of reasonable and occasionaly unreasonable use of force by police, it will be possible to establish a continuum for the use of force in various types of situations faced by law enforcement. This will help develop and refine the ability of an officer or a student of use of force to employ proper decision-making strategies and judgment regarding the use of force. This book develops a general use of force continuum with three basic levels of force—presence/communication, less lethal force, and lethal force—and examines how those levels can be utilized in different situations.

This book focuses primarily, although not exclusively, on federal constitutional requirements including federal statues and Supreme Court decisions. The federal constitution and the laws derived from it provide a "floor" of legal protection for all Americans and as a consequence, they provide basic standards in the application of force to which all law enforcement in the United States must be responsible. While states cannot provide less rights or protections than the federal constitution provides, they can and often do provide *more* protection than the federal constitution, providing more or enhanced rights to citizens compared with what the federal law requires. There are numerous cases regarding various aspects of police use of force at the federal and state level. We chose to focus on selected important cases for the purpose of this book and made editorial choices accordingly. A complete examination of cases regarding searches is beyond the scope of this book. So to gain a complete and accurate understanding of the particular legal constraints regarding arrest, search, and seizure, and other applications of the use of force, it is necessary to examine the state law for the jurisdiction in question. The variations in state law, however, make such an undertaking impractical in a book such as this. Various state laws are examined for illustrative purposes. Obviously, a state law enforcement officer must become familiar with his or her own state legal requirements regarding police use of force. In addition, knowledge of the specific policies of his or her agency and of the broader federal requirements is necessary.

Finally, it is also important to remember that technology, society, and law are constantly evolving and changing and often very rapidly. For example, Tasers are a relatively new less lethal technology and Tasers offer an important and useful alternative to firearms. Police use of Tasers is becoming more common as more and more departments recognize the possible benefits of an additional type of less lethal technology in the hands of their officers. In addition, Taser technology is evolving rapidly, with new types of the devices becoming available at a steady pace. And so, the law at multiple levels as well as departmental policies and guidelines regarding the use of Tasers are all evolving rapidly. Other new and as yet unforeseen technologies for the application of force by law enforcement will undoubtedly develop and be used by police for the security of our society. Developments in law usually follow developments in technology, not the other way around and laws, rules, and regulations will all evolve along with and subsequent to these new technologies.

The most basic and generalizable legal standard for the use of force is "reasonableness," and this book examines the reasonableness of use of force in a number of situations—both real and hypothetical—but what is reasonable today may well be eclipsed by the technology of tomorrow. Officers and other interested individuals will need to keep pace with these changes and maintain a current knowledge of federal and individual state law regarding use of force.

Questions for Discussion

Consider the following questions. How would you answer them?

1. How do most people view use of force by police? Favorably? Unfavorably?
2. How constrained should law enforcement be in its use of force? Are there too many constraints now or too few?
3. Who should determine whether the use of force by an officer is reasonable or justified? What role should citizens have in "policing the police"?
4. What should the balance be between the rights of the individual and the needs of society? Are rights being protected too much at the expense of safety and security?

Chapter One

Seizure, Searches, Probable Cause, and Arrest

Use of force issues most frequently arise during police interaction with individual citizens, although it is frequently not the direct application of physical force that most people think of as use of force. Events such as traffic stops, law enforcement responding to domestic violence disputes, or responding to other calls for assistance from individuals are interactions between law enforcement and the public that necessarily involve some use of force even if only at the lowest level, that of an official uniformed presence.[1] Many of these situations may begin as or evolve into situations that require additional, higher levels of force in the form of detention or seizure, any instance where a citizen or her property is detained or controlled by law enforcement for any length of time. If a citizen or her property is detained or seized, the Fourth Amendment and Supreme Court decisions interpreting that amendment are implicated and there are foundational legal rules that must be understood, considered, and addressed by the individuals exercising that use of force. The Fourth Amendment to the United States Constitution provides the foundation for all federal and therefore ultimately all state laws regarding arrest, search, and seizure.

The Fourth Amendment Standards

The Fourth Amendment is so fundamental in understanding and answering questions of arrest, search, and seizure that any law enforcement officer would do well to memorize it. Should there be a civil or criminal trial arising from most uses of force by laws enforcement, defense attorneys will often rightly focus largely on Fourth Amendment issues. The Fourth Amendment provides that

> [t]he right of the people to be secure in their persons, houses, papers, and effects, against unreasonable searches and seizures, shall not be violated, and no Warrants shall issue, but upon probable cause, supported by Oath or affirmation, and particularly describing the place to be searched, and the persons or things to be seized.[2]

While it may be clear that unreasonable seizures and resultant searches are prohibited by the Fourth Amendment, the legal concept of seizure needs to be further explored. First, we need a working legal definition of the term "seizure." A legal seizure is simply a detention by police of an individual or her property, and removing that property from the control of the citizen or, in effect, taking control of the individual. On the basis of this definition of the formal legal concept of seizure, it is possible to derive and explore other important concepts such as search, arrest, and the exclusionary rule.

KEY DEFINITION 2—SEIZURE

Seizure is a broad concept including detentions, brief or lengthy, of property or people. The term implies the removal of something from the possession of another or removing the freedom of movement in the case of an individual being seized. A law enforcement officer may briefly seize or detain an individual and may do so with less than probable cause for purposes of a brief investigation. Higher standards are required to make full arrests.

An officer who stops a person for a traffic violation with the intent to issue that driver a simple citation and then lets the driver proceed has in fact engaged in a seizure. The traffic stop, including the presence of the uniform, the official vehicle, and the flashing lights, all these are a use of force by the officer to affect the seizure, however temporarily, of the driver, the car, and the car's occupants. While a full arrest might not occur in a traffic stop situation, a seizure, however minor and however temporary, has still occurred and force has been exercised by the officer. This type of minor or transitory seizure is limited in scope and effect and treated differently from the more significant seizures and detentions and traffic stops discussed in greater detail in Chapter Three, "Custodial Interrogation."

Beyond these simple and relatively uncontroversial seizures of individuals and their property, more serious exercises of force are often required of law enforcement. These may include "Terry Stops" based on reasonable suspicion and at the more significant end of the spectrum regarding seizures, officers may be required to make an arrest of an individual. The arrest is a much more serious and usually much longer-term seizure of the person than a simple traffic stop. The more serious and the longer the seizure, the greater the need for a higher standard of the officer involved. As we will see, arrests have significantly higher standards to which law enforcement must be responsible than do Terry Stops or simple traffic stops. Regardless of the scope of the seizure, however, officers must be aware of the relevant standards that constrain their behavior when seizing individuals or their property. As mentioned, those standards begin with and are all derived from the Fourth Amendment to the United States Constitution.

The Fourth Amendment and the Supreme Court decisions that interpret it apply to all seizures, regardless of how big or small, how temporary or long-term they are. All officers, lawyers, and judges must be familiar with the requirements of Fourth Amendment regarding seizures as well as how those standards have been interpreted by the Supreme Court, because when those rules are violated, the seizure, however useful to law enforcement or beneficial to society, may be held to be invalid and the fruits of that seizure, including any evidence found as a result, may be deemed to be inadmissible at trial. The legal rule that allows otherwise reliable evidence to be excluded from legal proceedings if that evidence was obtained through an improper, unconstitutional, or illegal seizure or search is known as the exclusionary rule.

The Exclusionary Rule

The exclusionary rule is well established in the American legal system. The Supreme Court in 1914 established a federal exclusionary rule in *Weeks v. United States* that remains largely unchanged till today.[3] Stated simply, the exclusionary rule provides that evidence seized as a result of an illegal search or seizure cannot be used against a defendant. For example, if police enter a home without probable cause, consent, or a warrant, and seizure of evidence occurs, then that evidence must be excluded from trial or other legal proceedings. Further, evidence found because of or as a result of the initial, illegally obtained evidence is also inadmissible, as it is considered tainted as "fruit of the poisonous tree."[4] Officers must therefore ensure that their actions in seizing and searching an individual or her property are legal under the Fourth Amendment. Failing to understand and properly apply the standards derived from the protections of the Fourth Amendment can have significant negative impacts.[5]

Obviously if evidence is excluded from trial on the basis of an improper seizure or search, a suspect, even a guilty suspect, might go free. This is one of the negative effects of the exclusionary rule. However, as there is no other meaningful remedy to prevent police from illegally seizing evidence, the exclusionary rule acts as an important check on the force that law enforcement can bring to bear on individuals in our society. The only other remedies available if illegally seized evidence were to be allowed to be admitted at a trial are *post factum* remedies involving civil or criminal actions against the officers who engaged in the illegal search after a defendant is convicted on the basis of improperly seized evidence. That type of action provides neither a real remedy for the person who has been wronged and imprisoned by the improper conduct—the individual wronged would still have been incarcerated—nor a meaningful deterrent against future improper action, though the system would have achieved its goal if only temporarily. So, the system is left with the exclusionary rule as the only meaningful deterrent and best remedy, and as a remedy the rule has assumed a preeminent place in American law.

KEY DEFINITION 3—EXCLUSIONARY RULE

> The rule requires that, "All evidence obtained by searches and seizures in violation of the Constitution is, by that same authority, inadmissible in a state court."[6]

The federal exclusionary rule found in *Weeks v. United States* was incorporated by the Supreme Court in *Mapp v. Ohio*. In that case, the Supreme Court took the rule found in *Weeks v. United* States, which had applied only to federal law enforcement, and required that all state officials be bound to the same standard. The facts of the incident that gave rise to the case are the following:

> On May 23, 1957, three police officers appeared at her (Ms. Mapp's) home and demanded entrance, explaining that they were searching for a man in connection with a recent bombing. After consulting with her attorney on the phone, Ms. Mapp told the officers she wouldn't admit them without a search warrant. Three hours later, the police officers returned, along with others, and forced their way into the house. Mapp followed behind them, demanding to see the search warrant. Finally, one of the officers produced a piece of paper that Mapp grabbed and shoved down the front of her blouse. The bombing suspect was not found, and the piece of paper turned out not to be a search warrant.[7]

Though the police did not find the man who they had alleged they were seeking, they did find material they considered obscene. That material was seized by the police during their search and eventually Ms. Mapp was convicted of possessing obscene materials. An appellate court affirmed the conviction, and Ms. Mapp appealed to the United States Supreme Court. The focus of the appeal was whether or not the First Amendment protected Ms. Mapp's possession of the allegedly obscene material although that was not the eventual basis of the decision by the Court.

The Supreme Court avoided the difficulties inherent in the obscenity question presented by the case. It chose instead to decide the *Mapp* case on broader grounds that included the Fourth Amendment. In deciding the case on these grounds, the Court incorporated provisions of the Fourth Amendment and announced the rule that illegally seized evidence must be excluded from trials held not just at the federal level but at the state level as well. Thus, the Supreme Court extended the constitutional protections of the exclusionary rule to persons accused in state courts as well as in federal courts.

There are of course exceptions to the exclusionary rule and many more battles have been fought over the exact meaning of the exclusionary rule since the Court decided *Mapp v. Ohio*. The exceptions that have been created are judicially recognized doctrines which, in some very specific circumstances, will allow tainted evidence to be admitted into a trial. These exceptions include doctrines of good faith, inevitable discovery, and independent source doctrine, among others. A full discussion of these technicalities is beyond the scope and purpose of this book. It is important to note, however, that these exceptions serve as an important means of ensuring that a balance is maintained between the need of the people to be secure in their persons and effects and the needs of law enforcement to perform the functions and duties that society demands of them. Good faith exceptions, exigent circumstance exceptions, and inevitable discovery exceptions have all changed the landscape of seizures and searches at both the federal and state levels and as technology and society continue to advance, additional exceptions to the exclusionary rule may well be developed in the law. A recent exception to the exclusionary rule involves the knock and announce rule and it illustrates the evolution of the exclusionary rule. The Supreme Court recently held that the exclusionary rule does not apply as a remedy to a failure to knock and announce before executing a warrant.[8] Though the exclusionary rule would not apply in a failure to knock and announce case, police could face civil liability for failure to knock and announce, in theory anyway. Despite the knock and announce decision and other limitations placed on the exclusionary rule, the rule still has teeth and meaning and can be disregarded only at one's own peril. There is a danger that a continued series of decisions like that on the knock and announce rule could so erode the exclusionary rule as to render it effectively meaningless. That however has not yet happened and is unlikely to occur. The exclusionary rule is likely to remain as a remedy and to be applied to cases in which police act in bad faith.

Exclusionary Rule Exceptions

The exclusionary rule represents a judicially imposed constraint on the admissibility of evidence, excluding it from consideration at trial in the determination of guilt. The rule is designed to deter or prevent police misconduct in investigating crimes—regardless of the benefit to society in solving crimes. Prior to the introduction of the exclusionary rule, evidence that was obtained illegally by the state was generally allowed to be introduced at trial if it met the general requirements for evidence, reliability and relevance. In *Weeks v. United States*, 232 US 383 (1914), the Supreme Court prohibited the use of illegally obtained evidence at trial. The general protections of the Fourth Amendment were extended to state actions (through the incorporation doctrine of the Fourteenth Amendment) in *Wolf v. Colorado*, 338 US 25 (1949) and the exclusionary rule was specifically incorporated in *Mapp v. Ohio*, 367 US 643 (1961). The exclusionary rule has been extended to include what is known as "derivative evidence," evidence that is indirectly obtained as a result of an illegal search or seizure. This idea is usually referred to as the "fruit of the poisonous tree" doctrine and it is intended to prohibit law enforcement from benefiting indirectly from illegal activity by generating subsequent, though related, evidence as a means of avoiding the exclusionary rule. Since the creation of the exclusionary rule in 1914, the Supreme Court has allowed that there are some specific exceptions to the general prohibition on utilizing illegally obtained evidence. Those exceptions are generally narrowly tailored to specific circumstances and are given careful review by the Supreme Court when they do arise.

Exception	Explanation and Limitations
Independent Source	"The 'independent source' doctrine permits the introduction of evidence initially discovered during, or as a consequence of, an unlawful search, but later obtained independently from lawful activities untainted by the initial illegality" (see *Silverthorne Lumber Co. v. United States*, 251 US 385). The source that provides the independent evidence or information necessary to secure a warrant or otherwise obtain the evidence legally must be entirely unconnected to the constitutional violation that otherwise produced the evidence. The Supreme Court explained the independent source exception in *Nix v. Williams*, 467 US 431 (1984). "By contrast, the independent source doctrine—allowing admission of evidence that has been discovered by means wholly independent of any constitutional violation rests on the rationale that society's interest in deterring unlawful police conduct and the public interest in having juries receive all probative evidence of a crime are properly balanced by putting the police in the same, not a worse, position that they would have been in if no police error or misconduct had occurred."
Attenuation	The attenuation exception allows for illegally obtained evidence to be admitted at trial even if no independent source exists if the means of obtaining the evidence are sufficiently remote from the primary illegality of the search or seizure. In *Nardone v. United States*, 308 US 338, 341 (1959), the Court explained that, "We need not hold that all

(continued)

Exception	Explanation and Limitations
	evidence is 'fruit of the poisonous tree' simply because it would not have come to light but for the illegal actions of the police. Rather, the more apt question in such a case is 'whether, granting establishment of the primary illegality, the evidence to which instant objection is made has been come at by exploitation of that illegality or instead by means sufficiently distinguishable to be purged of the primary taint.'" In *Brown v. Illinois*, 422 US 590 (1975), the Court clarified that there exist three factors in the determination of whether the original illegality has been sufficiently attenuated: 1) The time elapsed between the illegality and the evidence being obtained, 2) the presence of intervening circumstances, and 3) the flagrancy of the original illegality. The key question in determining attenuation is, "whether, granting establishment of the primary illegality, the evidence to which instant objection is made has been come at by exploitation of that illegality or instead by means sufficiently distinguishable to be purged of the primary taint" (see *Wong Sun v. United States*, 371 US 471 [1963]).
Inevitable Discovery	"The inevitable discovery doctrine, with its distinct requirements, is in reality an extrapolation from the independent source doctrine: Since the tainted evidence would be admissible if in fact discovered through an independent source, it should be admissible if it inevitably would have been discovered" (see *Murray v. United States*, 487 US 533 [1988]). In other words, if the evidence at issue would inevitably have been discovered as a result of normal and otherwise legal activities, the evidence is not considered 'fruit of the poisonous tree' and can be admitted at trial. The Court explained this exception further in *Nix v. Williams*, 467 US 431, writing, "[h]owever, if the government can prove that the evidence would have been obtained inevitably and, therefore, would have been admitted regardless of any overreaching by the police, there is no rational basis to keep that evidence from the jury in order to ensure the fairness of the trial proceedings. In that situation, the State has gained no advantage at trial and the defendant has suffered no prejudice. Indeed, suppression of the evidence would operate to undermine the adversary system by putting the State in a worse position than it would have occupied without any police misconduct."
Good Faith	In *United States v. Leon*, 486 US 897 (1984), the Supreme Court adopted a "good faith exception" to the exclusionary rule. This exception allows that when a law enforcement officer believes in good faith that he is acting legally, a subsequent showing of illegality will not necessarily cause the evidence to be excluded. This exception is applied primarily to searches pursuant to warrants that are found later to be defective. The Court explained that, "warrant issued by a detached and neutral magistrate but ultimately found to be invalid." It is important to note that the reliance by the officer

Exception	Explanation and Limitations
	must be an objectively reasonable reliance that is not a result of a judge acting as a "rubber stamp for the police" or having been misled by the officer in the affidavit for the warrant. The officer must also be relying on a warrant that is not so facially deficient, lacking the basic components of a valid warrant that no reasonable person would rely on it. The Court said, "A police officer's reliance on the magistrate's probable-cause determination and on the technical sufficiency of the warrant he issues must be objectively reasonable. Suppression remains an appropriate remedy if the magistrate or judge in issuing a warrant was misled by information in an affidavit that the affiant knew was false or would have known was false except for his reckless disregard of the truth, or if the issuing magistrate wholly abandoned his detached and neutral judicial role. Nor would an officer manifest objective good faith in relying on a warrant based on an affidavit so lacking in indicia of probable cause as to render official belief in its existence entirely unreasonable. Finally, depending on the circumstances of the particular case, a warrant may be so facially deficient—i.e., in failing to particularize the place to be searched or the things to be seized—that the executing officers cannot reasonably presume it to be valid" (see *United States v. Leon*, 486 US 897 [1984]).

In the case of Ms. Mapp, none of these exceptions to the exclusionary rule would have applied even if they had been recognized by the Court at that time. It does not appear that the officers involved were acting in good faith. They in fact gave Ms. Mapp a fake warrant. The possible exception of exigent circumstances does not apply here. If police were looking for a bombing suspect, exigent circumstances justifying their acting without a warrant would have been present. Yet police did not act with any apparent sense of urgency. Officers actually waited three hours before returning finally with a bogus warrant to search Ms. Mapp's residence. Such a delay certainly renders a claim of exigent circumstances unbelievable. The facts in *Mapp v. Ohio* represent a clear case of law enforcement, in pursuit of possibly legitimate goals and laudatory ends, overreaching and denying a citizen her reasonable rights under the Fourth Amendment.

As long as law enforcement acts within the Constitution and laws derived from it, the exclusionary rule and the technical exceptions to it should never come into play. The best practice is for an officer to know the law, both federal and jurisdiction-specific, and not seize or search individuals in violation of the Constitution or those laws. If the officer's actions in seizing and searching an individual are not legal, important evidence may not be admitted in the criminal case, and a guilty defendant *may* go free.

Reasonable Suspicion and the Terry Stop

Arrest is a much more serious and lengthy seizure of a person than incidents such as traffic stops or even significant seizures and searches as in the *Mapp* case. Thus, the legal requirements for arrest are higher than for a brief seizure that may or may not result in a subsequent search. Between the very brief seizure of a person as in a traffic stop and the very lengthy and serious seizure in arrest, lies a middle ground, the Terry Stop. The United States Supreme Court in *Terry v. Ohio*[9] considered the question of whether or not the police have the authority to briefly detain an individual for investigation purposes short of arrest. Ultimately in that case the Supreme Court ruled that a police officer can, in certain very specific circumstances, briefly detain an individual without the officer having sufficient probable cause to make an arrest, if the officer has a reasonable suspicion that the individual is up to no good. The judicially created standard of reasonable suspicion is a lower standard that the probable cause required for the longer and more serious seizure, that is, formal arrest.

KEY DEFINITION 4—REASONABLE SUSPICION

> Reasonable Suspicion is sufficient to provide Fourth Amendment justification for an officer temporarily seizing an individual provided that there is, "a particularized and objective basis, supported by specific and articuable facts, for *suspecting* a person of criminal activity."[10]

The following facts of *Terry v. Ohio* are classic. Officer McFadden, a veteran officer, became suspicious of two men in downtown Cleveland, at about 2:30 in the afternoon. The men appeared to be repeatedly and actively "casing" a store. Officer McFadden watched the men engage in this activity a number of times and the men appeared to report back to a third man nearby. Officer McFadden followed the three men and confronted them. He asked them their names and one man mumbled a response. Officer McFadden grabbed Terry and felt his shirt pocket area. Feeling a pistol, McFadden reached in and removed the gun. Officer McFadden then "patted-down" another man in the group and found a second gun. Terry was charged with carrying a concealed weapon. He moved to suppress the gun from evidence. The trial court denied the motion to suppress the gun and the court upheld Officer McFadden's search under a stop and frisk theory.[11]

On the basis of the facts outlined above, the officer was able to use his expertise and experience to substantiate a reasonable and articuable suspicion that the suspects were up to no good. It was that reasonable and articuable suspicion that motivated the stop and the temporary seizure of the individuals. During the stop, Officer McFadden uncovered evidence that established probable cause for arrest. Importantly, the Supreme Court allowed the officer's actions of initially stopping, or temporarily seizing, the suspects without sufficient probable cause for an arrest.

The Court ruled that, depending on the facts of each case, a police officer may conduct what has become known as a "Terry Stop," which can include a limited seizure and search including what has come to be known as a "pat-down" search.

KEY DEFINITION 5—"TERRY STOP"

"Where a police officer
1. Observes unusual conduct which leads him reasonably to conclude in light of his experience that criminal activity may be afoot and
2. That the persons with whom he is dealing may be armed and dangerous,

Where in the course of investigating this behavior he
1. Identifies himself as a policeman and
2. Makes reasonable inquiries, and

If nothing in the initial stages of the encounter serves to dispel his reasonable fear for his own or others' safety, he is entitled for the protection of himself and others in the area to conduct a carefully limited search of the outer clothing of such persons in an attempt to discover weapons which might be used to assault him. Such a search is a reasonable search under the Fourth Amendment, and any weapons seized may properly be introduced in evidence against the person from whom they were taken."[12]

In other words, where a police officer has a reasonable suspicion that criminal activity may be ongoing and where he has reasonable fear for his safety or the safety of others, he may briefly detain or seize the individuals he reasonably believes to be involved in that activity and ask questions of them. If the answers are not sufficient to allay the officer's reasonable fear that the individuals may be armed, the officer may, for purposes of his own protection and that of others, conduct a careful and limited search of the individuals.[13] A Terry Stop may well lead to the officer's formation of probable cause to make an arrest, depending on the circumstances. Evidence reasonably discovered during that search is generally admissible and not subject to exclusion at trial.

The Fourth Amendment requires probable cause for warrants, arrest, and for most seizures, by law enforcement. However, this type of Terry Stop is a permissible seizure and search under the Fourth Amendment, not based on probable cause, but rather a judicially created subcategory of cause called reasonable suspicion. As mentioned above, *reasonable suspicion* is a lower standard than probable cause as required for arrest but a higher standard than may be required for less significant, less lengthy, or less invasive seizures of an individual or his property. Other judicially created exceptions to the general requirement that law enforcement obtain a warrant also exist in the law and are outlined in the table below.

Exceptions to the Warrant Requirement

The Supreme Court of the United States has declared that "except in certain carefully defined classes of cases, a search of private property without proper consent is 'unreasonable' unless it has been authorized by a valid search warrant." (See *G. M. Leasing Corp. v. United States*, 429 US 338 [1977] quoting *Camara v. Municipal Court*, 387 US 523, 528–529) and that, "searches conducted outside the judicial process, without prior approval by judge or magistrate, are per se unreasonable under the Fourth Amendment—subject only to a few specifically established and well-delineated exceptions." (See *Carroll v. United States*, 267 US 132, 153, 156; *McDonald v. United States*, 335 US 451, 454–456; *Brinegar v. United States*, 338 US 160, 174–177; *Cooper v. California*, 386 US 58; *Warden v. Hayden*, 387 US 294). Because they are intended by the Supreme Court to be so narrowly tailored and because of the subjective nature of some aspects, these exceptions are often difficult to define in practice and should be relied up by law enforcement only in a carefully considered manner.

Border searches	"That searches made at the border, pursuant to the long-standing right of the sovereign to protect itself by stopping and examining persons and property crossing into this country, are reasonable simply by virtue of the fact that they occur at the border, should, by now, require no extended demonstration." *United States v. Ramsey*, (1977) (see also *Illinois v. Andreas*, 463 US 765 [1983]). A border search by customs or other official requires no warrant, no probable cause, nor any articuable suspicion to meet the reasonableness standard of the Fourth Amendment. They are generally presumed to be reasonable.
Consent searches	As with most rights, the Fourth Amendment right against searches may be waived in a voluntary and knowing manner by the suspect to be searched (see *Amos v. United States*, 255 US 313 [1921]; *Zap v. United States*, 328 US 624 [1946]; *Schneckloth v. Bustamonte*, 412 US 218 [1973]). An individual may consent to a search absent a warrant but the burden rests with the state to show, on the basis of a totality of the evidence, the suspect's awareness of the right against the search, and the voluntary nature of the waiver (see *Bumper v. North Carolina*, 391 US 543 [1968] and *Johnson v. United States*, 333 US 10 [1948]).
Exigent circumstances	Exigent circumstances require immediate action on the part of officers and may allow those officers to search an individual or his premises without a warrant, if there is an "indication that evidence would be lost, destroyed, or removed during the time required to obtain a search warrant" or, if because of those factors, a warrant could not easily and conveniently have been obtained. (See *Mincey v. Arizona*, 437 US 385 [1978].) These circumstances may also exist when law enforcement responds to a larger scale emergency situation. The seriousness of the crime being investigated (e.g., murder) does not, by itself, create the exigent circumstances necessary for a warrantless search absent other factors (see *Mincey v. Arizona*, 437 US 385 [1978]).
Incident to arrest	An officer may make a search of an individual and the area and effects under the immediate control of an individual incident to the arrest of that individual (*see Weeks v. United States*, 232 US 383 [1914]; *Carroll v. United States*, 267 US 132 (1925); *Agnello v. United States*, 269 US 20 [1925]). The validity of a warrantless search incident to arrest rests on the underlying validity of the arrest itself, and that validity may not rest on the fruits of the warrantless search.
Open fields	The Supreme Court has declared that "it is enough to say that, apart from the justification, the special protection accorded by the Fourth Amendment to the people in their 'persons, houses, papers and effects,' is not extended to the open fields. The distinction between the latter and the house is as old as the

(continued)

common law". *Hester v. United States*, 265 US 57 (1924). Further, in *Oliver v. United States*, 466 US 170 (1984), the Court clarified further that "[t]he government's intrusion upon open fields is not one of those 'unreasonable searches' proscribed by the Amendment" and that "an individual may not legitimately demand privacy for activities conducted out of doors in fields, except in the area immediately surrounding the home." This has been extended to outbuildings that are visible (even if only to trespassers in *United States v. Dunn*, 480 US 294 (1987).

Plain view

Whenever an officer observes something illegal which is held out to the public, or, if the officer is somewhere he has a right to be and observes something illegal in plain view, he may determine probable cause and arrest the individual and seize the evidence without a warrant. There is no reasonable expectation of privacy to something in plain view (see *Harris v. US*, 390 US 234 [1947] and *Washington v. Chrisman*, 455 US 1 [1982]). The Court put it clearly in *Katz v. United States*, 389 US 347 (1967), that "[w]hat a person knowingly exposes to the public, even in his own home or office, is not a subject of Fourth Amendment protection. See *Lewis v. United States*, 385 US 206, 210; *United States v. Lee*, 274 US 559, 563. But what he seeks to preserve as private, even in an area accessible to the public, may be constitutionally protected. See *Rios v. United States*, 364 US 253; *Ex parte Jackson*, 96 US 727, 733."

Plain feel

The exception provides that where officers feel an object in the course of legitimate police conduct such as a Terry Stop, this provides probable cause for a further search or seizure. In such a case, the further intrusion need not be authorized by a warrant because it is predicated on the legitimacy of the initial intrusion. The Court made this exception explicit in *Minnesota v. Dickerson*, 508 US 366 (1993), when it declared that "[t]he police may seize non-threatening contraband detected through the sense of touch during a protective pat-down search of the sort permitted by Terry, so long as the search stays within the bounds marked by Terry."

Special needs

A claim to a special needs exception generally requires a case by case analysis by a court to determine the legitimacy of the warrantless search. There are, however, some generally recognized types of searches that fall into this category. Administrative searches in prisons and for the purposes of overseeing individuals on probation do not require a warrant (see *Hudson v. Palmer*, 468 US 517 [1984] and *Griffin v. Wisconsin* 483 US 868 [1987]). It is important that a generalized interest in reducing crime or protecting society is not a special need in this context and that a special need is "divorced from

	the State's general interest in law enforcement" (see *Ferguson v. City of Charleston* 532 US 67 [2001]).
Terry Stop	"Where a police officer 1. Observes unusual conduct which leads him reasonably to conclude in light of his experience that criminal activity may be afoot and 2. That the persons with whom he is dealing may be armed and dangerous, Where in the course of investigating this behavior he 1. Identifies himself as a policeman and 2. Makes reasonable inquiries, and if nothing in the initial stages of the encounter serves to dispel his reasonable fear for his own or others' safety, he is entitled for the protection of himself and others in the area to conduct a carefully limited search of the outer clothing of such persons in an attempt to discover weapons which might be used to assault him. Such a search is a reasonable search under the Fourth Amendment, and any weapons seized may properly be introduced in evidence against the person from whom they were taken" (see *Terry v. Ohio,* 392 US 1 [1968]).
Vehicle exception	Vehicles may, in many cases be searched without a warrant based on two separate rationale. In *Carroll v. United States,* 267 US 132 (1925), that vehicles may be searched without a warrant if the officer undertaking the search has probable cause to believe that the vehicle contains contraband. The Court explained that the mobility of vehicles would allow them to be quickly moved from the jurisdiction if time were taken to obtain a warrant. That mobility argument has been supplemented by the court asserting in *Cardwell v. Lewis,* 417 US 583 (1974), that "One has a lesser expectation of privacy in a motor vehicle because its function is transportation and it seldom serves as one's residence or as the repository of personal effects. . . . It travels public thoroughfares where both its occupants and its contents are in plain view."

Probable Cause and Arrest

Probable cause is more stringent standard than a reasonable suspicion. It is the standard necessary for the most significant types of seizures of an individual including arrest, and may be determined to exist in two separate ways. An officer observing a crime being committed in his or her presence has established probable cause and can proceed to seize, detain, and even arrest the individual. Probable cause can be determined by a judge on the basis of other evidence submitted to her by an officer or by a prosecuting attorney. In most cases, it is preferable, when practical, that a judge determines probable cause for an arrest or search in advance. The nature of law enforcement makes such advance judicial determinations, however desirable, sometimes impractical. In cases where an officer faces exigent circumstances it is likely to fall to that officer on the scene to make probable cause determinations.

KEY DEFINITION 6—PROBABLE CAUSE

> **Probable cause is a set of trustworthy facts or information which objectively gives the officer or judge a reasonable belief that a crime *likely* is being committed or *likely* has been committed. Those facts need not be sufficient to establish guilt but they must be more than mere suspicion. Probable cause necessary for arrest and seizures and searches is greater than the reasonable suspicion that a crime might be committed necessary for Terry Stops.**

In many instances, a law enforcement officer in the field can and will have to be responsible for determining whether there is sufficient probable cause for seizure, search, or arrest of an individual or her property. Doing so, however, is not without risk and it is generally preferable to have a competent court review the evidence of probable cause and issue a warrant a priori. In the absence of a warrant, when the officer has to determine herself whether or not probable cause exists, problems can easily arise. Even if the probable cause seems clear to the officer on the scene and in the moment, a court may later disagree and that may result in the seizure, search, or arrest being held void by that court. Consider the facts from the following case:

> Reliable informant Khoury told a federal postal inspector that Watson had supplied him with a stolen credit card and had agreed to furnish additional cards at their next meeting, scheduled for a few days later. At that meeting, which occurred in a restaurant, Khoury signaled the inspector that Watson had the cards, at which point the inspector arrested Watson without a warrant, as he was authorized to do under 18 U.S.C. Section 3061 and applicable postal regulations. The court of appeals held the arrest unconstitutional because the inspector had failed to secure an arrest warrant, although he concededly had time to do so, and this was a significant factor in the court's additional holding that Watson's subsequent consent to a search of his car was not voluntary.[14]

In considering the above facts, the question presented to the Court was whether the federal officer was required to obtain an arrest warrant before effectuating the arrest or, could the officer make the probable cause determination on his own. In other words, did the above facts constitute probable cause for Watson's arrest by the officer in the absence of a judicial predetermination that such probable cause existed? The Court of Appeals found that the officer did indeed need to have a warrant in hand in this case primarily because he had sufficient time to obtain such a warrant before the arrest. In reversing that decision, the Supreme Court said:

> Law enforcement officers may find it wise to seek arrest warrants where practicable to do so, and their judgments about probable cause may be more readily accepted where backed by a warrant issued by a magistrate .... But we decline to transform this judicial preference into a constitutional rule when the judgment of the Nation and Congress has for so long been to authorize warrantless public arrests on probable cause rather than to encumber criminal prosecutions with endless litigation with respect to the existence of exigent circumstances, whether it was practicable to get a warrant, whether the suspect was about to flee, and the like. [15]

The Supreme Court clearly held in this case that an officer may make decisions about probable cause and make arrests on the basis of those decisions and can do so even when he has sufficient time to obtain a warrant in advance of the arrest. However, the Court clearly also believed that "[the officer's] judgments about probable cause may be more readily accepted where backed by a warrant issued by a magistrate." Officers then should be careful that they do not overuse their individual abilities to determine and evaluate whether or not probable cause exists. They should instead rely, when practical, on judicially issued warrants for arrests.

When it is reasonable, a judge can and often should predetermine probable cause when granting a warrant. In such cases, the officer requesting the warrant for arrest or search submits an affidavit of probable cause detailing all the facts that the officer believes establishes the existence of probable cause. The judge then evaluates the affidavit, possibly questions the officer, and either agrees or disagrees with the assessment of the officer. The grant or denial of a warrant follows from this. This judicial review of the facts supporting the assertion of probable cause helps to insure the legality of the officer's subsequent arrest or search. The process also significantly diminishes the possibility of officer error or that the seizure, search, or arrest will be held void in subsequent court proceedings. It is always wise to get an arrest and or search warrant where possible; the warrant amounts to prior judicial approval for the exercise of force in seizure, search, or arrest, approval that will usually be upheld by subsequent actors. Prior judicial approval protects the officer and the case that the officer is building; it also makes it harder for the subject of the arrest, seizure, or search to argue later that some form of the exclusionary rule should come into play.

Even in the absence of a warrant, law enforcement is frequently called upon to act very quickly and to make decisions that are nearly instantaneous. Often these split-second decisions arise as the result of what are known as "exigent circumstances." This is a term that arises often in discussions about arrest, search, and seizure issues. The law recognizes that sometimes, where there are exigent or emergency circumstances, law enforcement officers need to act without a warrant to seize suspects or evidence. For instance, if a suspect is firing a gun at people, police will not certainly have to take time to get prior judicial approval and a warrant to arrest the perpetrator. The presence of exigent circumstances can excuse officers from getting a warrant without significantly damaging the case the officer is building or without jeopardizing the arrest. The circumstances, however, must truly be exigent and claiming exigency when none truly exists will not work as an excuse or as a means to get around the requirements of probable cause or warrants. For example, police may enter a house without a warrant to break up a fight in which injuries have occurred or could occur; the fight creates an exigent circumstance, known as the "emergency aid" exception, which allows police to enter without a warrant.[16] The presence or absence of exigent circumstances is likely be judged by courts, judges, and even by the media after the fact by what is known as the "objectively reasonable" standard. So if officers are going to act on the basis of exigency, they should be confident that a "reasonable person" will consider their actions appropriate and the circumstances truly exigent.

KEY DEFINITION 7—EXIGENT CIRCUMSTANCES

Exigent circumstances are *emergency circumstances* in which time is of the essence and there is imminent danger to people or possibly to evidence. In seizure and arrest, this usually refers to situations in which the officer would be unable to effectuate the arrest or seize the necessary evidence unless they act swiftly and without prior judicial approval.

Whether undertaken by an officer on the basis of her perception of probable cause or after the issuance of a warrant, or even in exigent circumstances, the police in some circumstances must seize individuals in a more serious and longer-term fashion, and exercise a use of force that amounts to an "arrest."

KEY DEFINITION 8—ARREST

Arrest is a narrower concept than seizure; it is a specific and very serious kind of seizure. All that is required is some affirmative action by the officer to detain or to take actual control of the person. Arrest is said to have occurred when a reasonable person would feel that, having been detained, he or she was not free to leave or otherwise decline the officer's request.[17]

"Arrest," as in most legal determinations, depends on the circumstances. Because it is situational, "arrest" is a complicated term to define before it occurs. The fact of an arrest must be determined by considering the totality of the circumstances of the seizure of the individual. Despite portrayals in the popular media, the law considers that a person can in fact be under arrest, even if the officer never says the individual is under arrest. In the following case, it is clear that the individual was legally under arrest despite the fact that he was never declared to be so by the officers. He was clearly not free to leave and had no option but to comply with the request of the officers involved.

Police, investigating the murder of a 14-year-old girl and went to the house of a 17-year-old suspect. When they arrived, the police did not have sufficient probable cause or a warrant to arrest the suspect. Despite that fact,

six police officers went to his home in the middle of the night and, after his father allowed them in, roused him from his bed by shining a flashlight on him. "We need to go and talk," one officer said, to which the teenager replied, "O.K." The officers then handcuffed him and took him to the police station, barefoot and in his underwear. There, after receiving his Miranda warnings, he implicated himself in the murder.[18]

It may seem obvious that a reasonable person in the circumstances described above, would consider himself under arrest, or seized within the meaning of the Fourth Amendment. The Texas Appeals Court, however, disagreed with that obvious interpretation of the events. That court argued that because the officers had never informed the teen that he was "under arrest," he had actually been free to leave at any time and did not have to implicate himself in the crime.

The United States Supreme Court was outraged by the decision of the Texas Appeals Court. The Supreme Court, in overturning the decision of the Texas Appeals Court, said, "A group of police officers rousing an adolescent out of bed in the middle of the night with the words 'we need to go and talk' presents no option but 'to go.'" "It was 'beyond cavil' that Mr. Kaupp had been arrested, and arrested unconstitutionally without either a warrant or probable cause, the court said."[19] Clearly the 17-year-old was arrested.

The Texas case is an extreme example and, because of the absence of sufficient probable cause determined by the officers or by a court through the issuance of a warrant, obviously an illegal arrest. However in some cases where the facts are less clear cut, reasonable minds can differ regarding when or whether circumstances would lead a reasonable person to believe that he is not free to go or otherwise terminate the encounter. To protect himself and his seizure or arrest, an officer has to consider the totality of the circumstances of his encounter with the suspect. Information such as where the encounter occurs, whether at the suspect's home or in public, whether on the street or in a crowded bus is important for determining whether a detention is an arrest and even if it is reasonable. While the place of the detention is important and relevant, the length of the detention is a weightier factor. The place of the detention does matter; one generally has the highest expectation of privacy and freedom from intrusion in the home, versus a generally lesser expectation of privacy in public.

Other factors such as the length of the detention and the reasons for the detention will also come into play in determining whether the temporary seizure or detention has met the legal definition of an arrest—the longer the detention, the more serious it is and the more likely it will be considered an arrest. Finally the presence of a warrant or reasonable probable cause or reasonable suspicion will determine whether the detention is ultimately viewed as an arrest and as a legally valid one in subsequent proceedings, should they occur. The bottom-line question that an officer should ask himself is whether he would feel reasonably free to leave or terminate the encounter if he were in the suspect's shoes. If the answer is "no," then it is likely that the officer has applied sufficient force for the arrest to occur.

In some instances it may be reasonable for an officer to mitigate some of these issues surrounding questions of detentions as arrests. An officer could choose to explicitly inform the suspect about the seizure or detention. A statement such as "you are not under arrest and you have a right to leave, ending this encounter, or you can talk with me" would make subsequent claims about whether or not an arrest had occurred much easier to unravel. A notice of this type should create a presumption that the stop is not an arrest and that subsequent discussion is voluntary and that no reasonable person would assume that an arrest had occurred. Such a warning is tantamount to an officer seeking consent. Currently such a warning is not required by law, but it could prove useful in many situations. Certainly if the officer has a reasonable suspicion, the officer can briefly detain the suspect pursuant to *Terry*. Or if the officer has probable cause, the officer can arrest the individual. A warning of this type might provide a means for an officer to accomplish his objectives despite having neither sufficient reasonable suspicion nor probable cause.

Officers have another crucial tool in investigating criminal activity, a tool that may resolve many of the issues discussed above. That tool is consent. An individual can consent to waive *any* constitutional right that they have and thereby consent to the application of force by the officer, provided that the consent is proper.

KEY DEFINITION 9—CONSENT

> **Consent involves an agreement or willingness on the part of the individual that an invasion of a right may occur. A person can waive any constitutional right that they have, if that waiver is made knowingly, intelligently, and voluntarily.[20]**

This means that a person can waive their right, the legal requirement, and concede that officers who have a reasonable suspicion, probable cause, or a warrant, to seize or search them or their property can do so as long as that waiver is freely given. The waiver does not have to be wise and individuals are free to act against their own best interest in providing consent and waiving rights. However, and very importantly, consent to waive rights can never be unduly coerced. Issues surrounding consent are addressed in greater detail in Chapter Five, on "Custodial Interrogation." Obtained and used properly, consent is one of the most powerful investigatory tools that officers have, but the burden to prove that consent was not coerced will always be on the law enforcement personnel who obtained the waiver of rights. People often consent to waive their rights and allow seizures, searches, and interrogations.

Privacy Expectations and Constitutional Law

Issues of privacy are central in instances of arrest, search and seizure. As we have seen, the Fourth Amendment generally requires a warrant before police can arrest, search, or seize someone or something. The Supreme Court, in various cases and in various ways, has recognized a person's right to privacy.[21] This is important for police because if an individual has a reasonable expectation of privacy and the police exercise force such as in detention, seizure, or arrest in a manner that interferes with that reasonable expectation of privacy without lawful grounds, the exclusionary rule may apply and important evidence may again be lost. If, on the other hand, a person does not have a reasonable expectation of privacy in some specific instance, then police may not need a warrant at all to exercise force through seizures, searches, or arrests. There are two Supreme Court cases that are of crucial importance in understanding privacy as it relates to these issues. The first case recognizes a general right to privacy but also acknowledges that police generally do need warrants to exercise some of these types of force suggesting that there are significant limitations on a general expectation of privacy by the individual. The second case recognizes the impacts that technology is having on society and that as technology is constantly changing and evolving, an individual's reasonable expectations of privacy are also changing and even eroding.

In a landmark case, *Katz v. United States*, the Supreme Court acknowledged an individual right regarding privacy but also took pains to carefully describe some important limits on that right.[22] The Court made it clear in Katz that "the Fourth Amendment protects people, not places." What a person knowingly exposes to the public, even in his own home or office, is not a subject of Fourth Amendment protection. … But what he seeks to preserve as private, even in an area accessible to the public, may be constitutionally protected. In simplest terms, the Court has created a rule regarding privacy as it relates to seizures and searches. When an individual is seeking to hide something, even if in a relatively public location, he has a higher expectation of privacy there than if he leaves something out in the open, even if he does so in a private and inaccessible place. This rule, as do many others, cuts two ways. Certainly after *Katz*, individuals can have a right to privacy under many circumstances and police in those circumstances would need warrants to search or seize people or property. But, the ruling in *Katz* also establishes the famous "plain view rule."

KEY DEFINITION 10—PLAIN VIEW

> Whenever an officer observes something illegal which is held out to the public, or, if the officer is somewhere he has a right to be and observes something illegal in plain view, he may determine probable cause and arrest the individual and seize the evidence without a warrant. There is no reasonable expectation of privacy to something in plain view.[23]

It may not always be clear under what circumstances an officer must get a warrant before searching, or what constitutes a search. It is clear, however, that objects or actions maintained or undertaken in plain view provide a clear basis for probable cause for purposes of seizure, search, and even arrest.

Beyond that simple rule, however, determining what constitutes a reasonable expectation of privacy is challenging. Consider the following question: Does one have a reasonable expectation of privacy in their garbage? Many would answer "yes," and say that individuals do or at least should have a reasonable expectation of privacy in their garbage and many might suggest that the rule in *Katz* would provide some basis for that response. Reasonable minds could disagree on whether or not, and under what circumstances, a reasonable expectation of privacy in garbage exists. The Supreme Court has actually considered and answered this question.[24]

> In early 1984, Investigator Jenny Stracner of the Laguna Beach Police Department received information indicating that respondent Greenwood might be engaged in narcotics trafficking ...
>
> On April 6, 1984, Stracner asked the neighborhood's regular trash collector to pick up the plastic garbage bags that Greenwood had left on the curb in front of his house and to turn the bags over to her without mixing the contents with garbage from other houses. The trash collector ... collected the garbage bags from the street in front of Greenwood's house, and turned the bags over to Stracner. ... She recited the information that she had gleaned from the trash search in an affidavit in support of a warrant to search Greenwood's home.
>
> Police officers encountered both respondents at the house later that day when they arrived to execute the warrant. The police discovered quantities of cocaine and hashish during their search of the house. Respondents were arrested on felony narcotics charges.[25]

The Superior Court found that the above warrantless search violated the Fourth Amendment, and the Court of Appeals agreed that the warrantless search was in violation of the Fourth Amendment. The Supreme Court disagreed and held that "having deposited their garbage 'in an area particularly suited for public inspection and, in a manner of speaking, public consumption, for the express purpose of having strangers take it,' respondents could have had no reasonable expectation of privacy in the inculpatory items that they discarded."

Legal analysts, lawyers, and others disagree about the Supreme Court decision upholding the warrantless search of Greenwood's garbage. Officer Stracner could have obtained a warrant before searching Greenwood's garbage and, if she had obtained a valid warrant, no one would have questioned the constitutionality of police action in the Greenwood case. It was a risky move to search Greenwood's garbage without a warrant. The trial court and appeals court threw the evidence out because they thought police should have obtained a warrant before searching. Only a final intervention by a divided Supreme Court saved the day for the Laguna Beach Police Department. The Greenwood precedent may not stand the test of time as it stands on what many consider to be shaky legal reasoning. Again, the best practice for any law enforcement officer is, when in doubt and when possible, is to get a warrant before searching or seizing. Failing to do so may mean that the exclusionary rule will apply and the case may be in considerable legal jeopardy.

While searching the trash of a suspect may be a decidedly low-tech approach, other forms of technology have become complicating issues in determining what constitutes a reasonable expectation of privacy. Technological advancements have given rise to questions that are clearly not contemplated by the original text of the Fourth Amendment or by previous Supreme Court decisions. One area of technological growth with clear implications for the use of force to seize and search is the field of electronic surveillance. It is not clear whether police need a warrant to use electronic surveillance technology in all cases or even in what types of cases. The answer depends, as it so often does, on the circumstances. Consider the following case:

> In 1991 Agent William Elliot of the United States Department of the Interior came to suspect that marijuana was being grown in the home belonging to petitioner Danny Kyllo, part of a triplex on Rhododendron Drive in Florence, Oregon. Indoor marijuana growth typically requires high-intensity lamps. In order to determine whether an amount of heat was emanating from [Kyllo's] home consistent with the use of such lamps, at 3:20 a.m. on January 16, 1992, Agent Elliot and Dan Haas used an Agema Thermovision 210 thermal imager to scan the triplex. Thermal imagers detect infrared radiation, which virtually all objects emit but which is not visible to the naked eye. The imager converts radiation into images based on relative warmth—black is cool, white is hot, shades of grey connote relative differences; in that respect, it operates somewhat like a video camera showing heat images. The scan of Kyllo's home took only a few minutes and was performed from the passenger seat of Agent Elliot's vehicle across the street from the front of the house and also from the street in back of the house. The scan showed that the roof over the garage and a side wall of [Kyllo's] home were relatively hot compared to the rest of the home and substantially warmer than neighboring homes in the triplex. Agent Elliot concluded that [Kyllo] was using halide lights to grow marijuana in his house, which indeed he was. Based on tips from informants, utility bills, and the thermal imaging, a Federal Magistrate issued a warrant authorizing a search of [Kyllo's] home, and the agents found an indoor growing operation involving more than 100 plants. [Kyllo] was indicted on one count

of manufacturing marijuana, in violation of 21 U.S.C. Section 841(a) (1). He unsuccessfully moved to suppress the evidence seized from his home and then entered a conditional guilty plea.[26]

Justice Scalia summed up the question presented. He wrote that "[t]his case presents the question of whether the use of a thermal-imaging device aimed as a private home from a public street to detect relative amounts of heat within the home constitutes a 'search' within the meaning of the Fourth Amendment."[27] In its opinion, the Supreme Court argued, "[w]e think that obtaining by sense-enhancing technology any information regarding the interior of the home that could not otherwise have been obtained without physical 'intrusion into a constitutionally protected area' ... constitutes a search—at least where (as here) the technology in question is not in general public use."[28]

This rule from the Supreme Court does not offer good practical guidance to police regarding whether they must get a warrant before using an electronic surveillance device. The Supreme Court said essentially that police need a warrant to use a thermal-imaging device or other similar devices that are intended to avoid physical intrusion into the home, unless that device is in the general public use. So there appears to be an undefined general public use exception to the requirement that police get a warrant before using such a device. Among other problems in this particular case was the fact that there were actually thousands of these devices in use, and some were easily available to the public for rent through an 800-number. Once again, it is clear that for law enforcement officers in the field, erring on the side of caution and obtaining a warrant when possible before exercising force through searches and seizures provides the maximum assurance that the search, seizure, or evidence obtained will not be disallowed by a court at a later date.

All this leaves the question of when an officer does or does not need a warrant before exercising force in a search of an individual or her possessions somewhat murky. An individual's reasonable expectation of privacy has direct implications for warrant requirements, and those in turn directly determine whether an officer must get warrants before seizure and search and this again depends ultimately on the totality of the circumstances. Generally if a reasonable officer would say there are exigent circumstances, such as a crime being committed in the officer's presence that justify acting without a warrant and the officer can determine probable cause, then an officer does not need one. However, it is always the best practice, if circumstances allow, to get a warrant from a judge before acting, and when in doubt, officers should always attempt to get a warrant. This is doubly true when dealing with a big case, a complex or technologically driven case or, indeed, any case the officer really does not want to lose. Failing to obtain a warrant before the application of force through the search or seizure increases the risk of having evidence thrown out because of the exclusionary rule. Acting with a warrant certainly does not guarantee that any evidence will be admissible, but it goes a long way in getting the evidence admitted in court and in building a solid case against the accused.

Ethics and Discretion

Society trusts police officers to uphold the law and protect it from criminal elements. It is the greatest trust that society can repose, and it is one of the reasons why police officers take an oath to uphold the law.[29] That oath affirms that the United States is a nation of laws and no person is above the law, not even those who enforce it. No one in the military or law enforcement swears allegiance to a person; all swear to uphold the Constitution of the United States and the laws that are made pursuant thereto. Society trusts its law enforcement officers to exercise wise judgment and discretion in carrying out their duties. As police and other law enforcement are often all that stand between law-abiding elements and criminal elements, and as police often respond to crimes in progress or to crime scenes, police officers have a tremendous amount of power. With that power—the power to seize people, cars, or other property, the power to search individuals or their property, the power to detain and arrest, the power to use lethal force if circumstances warrant—comes responsibility. Society expects police officers to use their power for the greater good and to act in good faith. It should be every police officer's goal to live up to the trust placed in them and to use their power wisely and justly for the greater good. Police officers are professionals and as such they should be the first to police themselves for ethical behavior. Each officer's behavior reflects upon all law enforcement officers. If one officer is not ethical or credible, he or she taints and tarnishes all law enforcement officers to some degree. So, inappropriate behavior needs to be appropriately addressed and dealt with as soon as possible. Otherwise, an isolated problem can grow into a huge one. The media and/or the courts may get involved, and that might be a good and necessary thing in some circumstances, for they are the ultimate checks against police abuses of power.

As professionals, police officers should strive to improve themselves and their professional knowledge. Professionalism and ethics should regularly be discussed.[30] Experience, training, and education help to make one wiser. Veteran officers should mentor younger officers, and younger officers should not assume that they know everything; they should listen to advice from veteran officers. All departments should have policy and procedure manuals with which their officers should be familiar. These policy and procedure manuals should be regularly updated as should the department's use of force continuum. All departments should provide regular training in the use of force, and updates on changes in the law. As reasonableness is the cornerstone of our legal system, "reasonable" should be the watchword for all police policies, procedures, and actions, particularly in the areas of search, seizure, and arrest.

One final note regarding discretion in these areas: while there is no substitute for knowledge about the law and proper procedures, officers have to follow their gut instinct and pay close attention to the circumstances and act prudently. If something does not seem right, then officers must proceed accordingly. It is better that an officer be safe and remove themselves from the situation, get a warrant, and or wait for proper backup before proceeding than to have evidence suppressed, arrests voided, or guilty suspects go free.

Questions for Discussion

Consider the following questions. How would you answer them?

1.   Is the exclusionary rule a good thing or a bad thing? Does it hamper law enforcement more than is necessary or is it a protection for basic rights?

2. Are warrant requirements too restrictive? Should officers have increased discretion to act on their own without fear of having evidence excluded?

3. How important are ethics for law enforcement officers? How can ethical behavior be valued, taught, trained, and maintained by agencies and officers?

4. What should be the penalty for officers who willfully act in an unethical manner? Who should be responsible for making that determination?

Chapter Two

Use of Lethal
and Nonlethal Force

This chapter examines types of law enforcement actions that most people would recognize as "use of force" by police. This type of force, unlike the search and seizure discussed earlier, is the type of physical and dangerous force that is exercised up to and including the use of intentionally lethal force. This type of force, as with seizure or searches, is part of a larger continuum of force that is available to police officers in different situations. A complete definition of the idea of use of force must include the entirety of that continuum.

Consider again the Key definition of Use of Force given in the introduction:

KEY DEFINITION 1—USE OF FORCE (BY POLICE)

Use of Force by police is any expression of force that is meant to produce specific law-enforcement-related results. These expressions can include physical, uniformed police presence (at the minimal end of the continuum on use of force), flashing patrol car lights, foot or vehicle pursuit, use of fists and holds, batons, aerosols, Tasers, less lethal projectiles, water cannons, and firearms (at the maximum end of the continuum on use of force).

What type of force can or should be exercised in a given situation, or how far along the continuum it is reasonable and appropriate for an officer to go, is not an easy question to answer. Standards applied to search and seizures vary depending on factors such as how long the detention lasts or how in-depth the search is. The same is true when moving beyond simple seizures to more overt physical force. There are again several issues that an officer must consider when deciding what level of force, in this case explicitly physical force, to employ. As in Chapter One, these issues have been defined by the law, through the courts, and in departmental and agency policies and procedures.

Proportionality and Physical Force

Application of direct physical force is generally understood by the public to be use of force. Direct physical confrontations, particularly those that have the potential to result in grievous physical injury or death certainly gain the most media attention. However, perhaps this type of direct physical force is considerably less common than generally believed.[1] A study undertaken by the International Association of Chiefs of Police[2] came to four important conclusions about police use of physical force. First, the study found that police use physical force infrequently, in approximately 1% of their interactions with the public. Second, that when physical force is used, it is most frequently at the lowest end of the physical continuum and that 98% of arrests were made without the use of any weapon and the most common weapon used (in 1.2% of arrests) was only a chemical agent; firearms were used in only 0.2% of arrests. Third, those injuries resulting from use of force by law enforcement are most often minor: in 15% of use-of-force incidents resulting in any injury, the most common injuries reported were only cuts and bruises. Finally and fourth, use of physical force occurs most frequently when officers are attempting to make an arrest and a majority of the individuals who were subjected to physical force by officers admitted that their behavior may have caused the officer's response. A Bureau of Justice Statistics Report finds similar results in its 2005 survey, reporting that only 1.6 of the approximately 43.5 millions individuals who had contact with law enforcement had force used against them or were even threatened with the use of force.[3] It is generally only in the context of arrest or vehicle searches that physical force becomes necessary for officers and the discussion below assumes that general context.

When use of force by police is raised, the discussion frequently turns to questions of proportionality. Generally, proportionality requires that a threat be met only with an appropriate level of force in response. While the Supreme Court has been inconsistent regarding a legal requirement of proportionality in different contexts, fairness and the perception of fairness clearly require proportionality. Whether the force used by police in response to a threat was proportional or not is often a primary factor in the determination by courts or others concerning the reasonableness of that use of force. A disproportionately harsh response by police is likely to draw media scrutiny, public outrage, and possibly legal action. So, while it is important to consider proportionality in the application of force, it may often be very difficult to do so. There are few reliable data on the type, extent, and range of force that is used against officers in the field and as a result, it is often difficult to talk about clear-cut rules for proportionality.[4]

The use of physical force by police is typically considered within a use of force continuum. While considering use of force continuum, it is good to remember that use of force is situational and any continuum serves only as a general guideline. Use of force continuum can easily become overly complex in the attempt to be complete.[5] As an alternative, consider the three level reasonable use of force continuum, which employs the concept of proportionality, outlined below:

Reasonable Use of Force Continuum[6]

Level	Suspect Behavior	Reasonable Officer Response
One	Compliant with officer request(s)	Official presence, verbal communication, and commands
Two	Noncompliant, resistant, evasive, nondeadly threat to officer or others	Proportional and reasonable use of physical force possibly including less lethal weapons such as chemical agents or Tasers
Three	Imminent deadly threat or imminent great bodily harm threat to officer, self, or others.	Proportional and reasonable use of lethal force

For any use of force on the continuum, whether it contains three four or five levels, there is a single key question: Was police use of force objectively reasonable under the circumstances?

Use of Lethal Force

Lethal force is a type of force that is likely to cause death if employed and is therefore of great significance in the any understanding of use of force by law enforcement. However, while incidents involving use of lethal force are indeed important and often garner the most public and media scrutiny, they objectively represent only a small part of the use of force continuum and a small part of what law enforcement does.[7] The use of firearms is perhaps the most obvious example of lethal force used by police and therefore officers carrying firearms undergo extensive training in the use of those weapons at both the initial stages of their careers and generally in an ongoing fashion after that. That police officers have, as a matter of course, deadly force that is likely to cause death when employed at their disposal, raises the crucial question of when and under what circumstances an officer can use lethal force to make an arrest or deal with a noncompliant individual. As with many standards in law enforcement, the answer to when and how force can be employed varies considerably by jurisdiction and is controlled in different agencies to some degree by the policies and procedures of those agencies. There are, however, some overarching principles that may be as simple as a requirement that, if possible, the officer should give warning and yell something like "Police, Don't Move!"[8] Other requirements related to the use of explicitly lethal force can again be found in federal law and specifically in the interpretation of the Supreme Court. The Supreme Court case, *Tennessee v. Garner*, established one of the clearest legal rules regarding when and under what circumstances an officer can use specifically a firearm to stop an individual.

> At about 10:45 p.m. on October 3, 1974, Memphis Police Officers Elton Hymon and Leslie Wright were dispatched to answer a "prowler inside call." Upon arriving at the scene they saw a woman standing on her porch and gesturing toward the adjacent house. She told them she had heard glass breaking and that "they" or "someone" was breaking in next door. While Wright radioed the

dispatcher to say that they were on the scene, Hymon went behind the house. He heard a door slam and saw someone run across the back yard. The fleeing suspect, who was appellee-respondent's decedent, Edward Garner, stopped at a 6-feet-high chain link fence at the edge of the yard. With the aid of a flashlight, Hymon was able to see Garner's face and hands. He saw no sign of a weapon, and, though not certain, was "reasonably sure" and "figured" that Garner was unarmed. He thought Garner was 17 or 18 years old and about 5'5" or 5'7" tall. While Garner was crouched at the base of the fence, Hymon called out "police, halt" and took a few steps toward him. Garner then began to climb over the fence. Convinced that if Garner made it over the fence he would elude capture, Hymon shot him. The bullet hit Garner in the back of the head. Garner was taken by ambulance to a hospital, where he died on the operating table. Ten dollars and a purse taken from the house were found on his body.[9]

In the *Garner* case the Supreme Court found that the force utilized by Hymon was an application of lethal force not appropriate to apprehend the fleeing suspect. Perhaps one could predict the legal outcome of the case if one recognized the disproportional nature of the use of force (lethal force) by police to apprehend a fleeing felon (nonviolent) that presented no immediate (resistant, but not life-threatening) danger to anyone (on the basis of the use of force continuum presented above). The Supreme Court ruled:

> The use of deadly force to prevent the escape of all felony suspects, whatever the circumstances, is constitutionally unreasonable. It is not better that all felony suspects die than they escape. Where the suspect poses no immediate threat to the officer and no threat to others, the harm resulting from failing to apprehend him does not justify the use of deadly force to do so. It is no doubt unfortunate when a suspect who is in sight escapes, but the fact that the police arrive a little late or are a little slower afoot does not always justify killing the suspect. *A police officer may not seize an unarmed, non-dangerous suspect by shooting him dead.* (emphasis added)[10]

KEY DEFINITION 11—LETHAL FORCE (APPROPRIATE USE OF)

An officer can use deadly force only when he reasonably believes that his life or another's life is in danger, or if he reasonably believes that he or another faces grave bodily injury and that no reasonable alternative to the use of that force appeared to exist at the time.[11]

While the *Garner* decision makes it clear when lethal force may not be used by officers, it does not answer the question of how much force short of lethality may be employed. In other words, how much force can a police officer use to make an arrest or seizure? At first glance, the answer seems quite straightforward. The officer can use as much force as is necessary. But what does "necessary" mean in practice? The term "necessary" relates closely to the concepts of "reasonable" and "proportional." What force may reasonably be applied depends on the context in which that force is applied as well as the specific requirements of the jurisdiction in which the force is applied.[12] The level of force that is permissible must be arrived at considering the totality of the circumstances in which the officer finds himself or herself as well as the perception of the officer as it relates to alternative means of accomplishing the lawful ends intended by the force. In plain words, the officer can generally use the force necessary provided that such application of force is reasonable and proportional as required by the circumstances as he or she understands them at the time.[13] Officers employ the use of force to stop aggressive or noncompliant behavior. Put differently, law enforcement officers are not trained to shoot to kill; rather officers are trained to stop the threatening behavior. If officers use force, including deadly force, to compel compliance, then after the danger has subsided and it is safe to do so, officers should render and summon aid within a reasonable time to the subject or subjects of the officer's use of force.

KEY DEFINITION 12—DUTY TO RENDER AID
AFTER USE OF FORCE

> After use of force if it appears reasonably necessary to summon aid, then officers should render and summon appropriate aid within a reasonable time.

This definition raises again the term "reasonable" as a cornerstone of the law and of understanding use of force by law enforcement. Reason is the soul of the law and lawyers and judges almost always end up talking about, arguing about, and in the end deciding cases on the basis of reasonableness. If there is some situation not accounted for by the current law, then lawyers will often try to determine what would be reasonable or what a reasonable person might do under the circumstances. Ultimately law boils down to reasonableness and use of force issues are no different in that regard. The term "reasonable" will be the standard by which use of force conduct, either in a Terry Stop seizure or in a violent confrontation, will be measured and accepted or sanctioned. We need a working definition of the term "reasonable."

KEY DEFINITION 13—REASONABLE

"Fair, proper, just, moderate, or suitable under the circumstances," "not immoderate or excessive," "under the influence of reason, amenable to reason."[14]

Washington State law provides an example of "necessary" that is closely related to "reasonable." It contains RCW 9A.16.040 that addresses use of deadly force by police officers. This law defines the concept of necessary as it relates to the use of force as meaning that no reasonably effective alternative to the use of force appeared to exist and that the amount of force used was reasonable to affect the lawful purpose intended.[15] Clearly, the necessity, appropriateness, and permissibility of use of force are situational and the necessity of understanding the context may make the answer to specific questions very difficult. The terms "fair, proper, and just" in the above definition are the fulcrum when considering whether police use of force, deadly or otherwise, was allowable. If the action meets those criteria, then it is most probably allowable; if it fails to meet those criteria, then it is an incorrect and possible unlawful application of force. The law considers "reasonableness" from different perspectives and we should examine some important perspectives.

The law will often distinguish between "subjectively reasonable" and "objectively reasonable." Both, however, need to be considered when determining the use of force by an officer. When examining "subjective reasonableness" we have to take into consideration what the actor, the person using force, thinks about the use of force. Did he believe that what he was doing was "fair, proper, and just" or in other words, "reasonable." His statements about his perceptions are crucial. Did he believe, for instance, that he or others were in danger or serious danger? Did he believe that he faced the possibility of grave bodily injury if he did not apply that level or type of force? The subjective inquiry ends here. The subjective nature of this approach means that what the person applying the force believed must be taken at face value.

KEY DEFINITION 14—SUBJECTIVELY REASONABLE

An assessment of reasonableness based on what the actor believes to be or have been reasonable. If he believes that he acted reasonably then the action is subjectively reasonable.

When examining "objective reasonableness," we move away from what the actor himself thought at the time and ask what a hypothetical and reasonable person would have done or would consider proper in those circumstances. It is a different question from that of subjective reasonableness. While the law may consider subjective impressions in deciding questions surrounding use of force, it usually employs the "objectively reasonable" standard as the final measure when evaluating the use of force. The basic question for determining objective reasonableness is whether another reasonable person would have acted in a similar fashion in the same circumstances. This is a higher standard than subjective reasonableness, as one must consider what a reasonable person would have done; it does not assume that the actor was in fact a reasonable person. Objectively reasonable is the more common legal standard and the better standard.[16]

KEY DEFINITION 15—OBJECTIVELY REASONABLE

Objectively reasonable requires assessment by a third party to ask whether a hypothetically reasonable person in the actor's situation has acted as he did. This is a higher standard than subjectively reasonable, as one must consider what a reasonable person would have done—it does not assume that the actor was in fact a reasonable person. Objectively reasonable is the more common legal standard.[17]

An infamous case, the Bernhard Goetz case from the 1980s, illustrates the problems associated with subjective and objective interpretations of whether or not the use of force was reasonable.[18] Though Bernhard Goetz was a private citizen who used deadly force, his case is quite illustrative. Bernhard Goetz boarded a subway train car in New York City in 1984 and sat down in a nearly empty car. Four young men approached Goetz and one of the young men inquired of Goetz "'How are ya?' Canty and possibly a second youth, Barry Allen, then approached Goetz, and Canty asked him for five dollars. Goetz asked him what he wanted. Canty repeated: 'Give me five dollars.' Suddenly, the car resounded with gunshots, one aimed at each of the young blacks."[19] How should we evaluate the appropriateness of Goetz's use of force?

If we conduct a subjective inquiry, we ask what Goetz thought at the time he used deadly force? Did he believe he was in danger? Did Goetz believe it was appropriate to use deadly force? If Goetz answers "yes" to these questions, then subjectively his use of deadly force was reasonable. If subjective inquiry was all that was necessary, that answer would be sufficient to make the use of force appropriate. And that could be a big problem, as it would essentially amount to a rule that if one thinks it is appropriate to use deadly force, then it is fine. This could amount to a license to use deadly force whenever one subjectively feels as though it would be appropriate. So the subjective standard alone, while important, is problematic and can lead to unjust and inappropriate results.

If we inquire of the objective reasonableness of Goetz's actions, then we ask whether a reasonable person, in Goetz's circumstances, would have used deadly force as Goetz did. The objective inquiry is much different from and more complicated than the subjective inquiry. It requires that we evaluate the reasonableness of Goetz's actions under the circumstances. This is where the Goetz case gets to be very difficult and reasonable minds can differ on whether or not Goetz's use of force was reasonable and appropriate. Goetz gave conflicting statements. On the one hand, he indicated that he thought he was being mugged by these four men on a subway car. Four against one does certainly sound like a threat, and there was nowhere for Goetz to run. He was effectively cornered. But, was Goetz justified in pulling his gun and shooting his perceived attackers? Did Goetz knowingly create the situation and circumstances leading to the shootings? There is an argument that he was justified in using deadly force as he did under the circumstances. However, Goetz made a number of alarming statements regarding the shooting. He indicated that he knew that none of the four had a gun, and he wanted to make them suffer. He indicated at trial in a civil suit brought against him, that the mother of one of his attackers should have had an abortion.

His statements demonstrate considerable animus and are not consistent with the typical mens rea[20] in a case of self-defense. In a previous mugging incident, Goetz had pulled his gun, showed the gun, and had not fired it. The gun scared the attacker away. Did Goetz use his firearm too quickly or improperly in the subway car instance? Does it matter that he carried the gun illegally? Does it matter that after he fired a number of shots, he went back to an attacker and said something to the effect of "you appear to be all right, here's another," and fired again after the mugging was reasonably over? While the jury in the Goetz criminal case convicted him only of a weapons charge violation, the one in the subsequent civil action against Goetz did find him responsible for improperly using deadly force and awarded monetary damages of $43 million. Why was there a difference in outcomes in the criminal and civil trial? Well, one reason is the burden of proof. In a criminal case, the burden of proof is beyond a reasonable doubt, a very high standard; and the jury has to be unanimous in its verdict. In a civil case, the burden of proof is by a preponderance of the evidence (more likely than not), a much lower burden of proof. The jury in a civil case typically does not have to be unanimous in its verdict. Goetz did not take the witness stand in his criminal trial, but the jury did hear his taped confessions. Goetz did take the stand in his civil trial and made a number of inflammatory remarks, perhaps as he could not be tried criminally a second time for the shootings because of the double jeopardy clause of the Constitution. The jury heard from Goetz himself in the civil trial and evaluated his credibility and apparently rendered a judgment accordingly. Finally, it should be clear from considering the facts of the Goetz case that the answer to the question of reasonableness is difficult and subject to a fairly broad range of reasonable interpretations. Recognizing that may provide the best explanation for the differing outcomes in Goetz's criminal and civil trials and also a clear example of the difficulty of applying these standards in practice.

In use of force situations in particular and in criminal law issues in general, proportionality is a key concept in determining whether the officer acted properly or improperly. Looking back at the definition of "reasonable" and considering the characteristics of fairness, propriety, and justice, it should be clear that proportionality is a logical result of fairness, propriety, and justice. The absence of proportionality is necessarily the absence of fairness, propriety, and justice. So proportionality will almost always be a key issue in use of force inquiries. Internal and external reviewers, the media, and the jury will all at some point analyze whether the use of force was proportional to the threat encountered by police.

KEY DEFINITION 16—PROPORTIONALITY

> **Proportional means appropriate and fair. Proportional action is action that fits the circumstance, action that was appropriate to the circumstance. A proportional response is in proper relationship to the event.**

The Supreme Court provided further guidance regarding how to determine whether use of force by police was reasonable.[21] Consider the following facts:

> Respondent Connor, an officer of the Charlotte, North Carolina, police Department, saw Graham hastily enter and leave the store. The officer became suspicious that something was amiss and followed Berry's car. About one-half mile from the store, he made an investigative stop. Although Berry told Connor that Graham was simply suffering from a "sugar reaction," the officer ordered Berry and Graham to wait while he found out what, if anything had happened at the convenience store. When Officer Connor returned to his patrol car to call for backup assistance, Graham got out of the car, ran around it twice, and finally sat down on the curb, where he passed out briefly.
>
> In the ensuing confusion, a number of other Charlotte police officers arrived on the scene in response to Officer Connor's request for backup. One of the officers rolled Graham over on the sidewalk and cuffed his hands tightly behind his back, ignoring Berry's pleas to get him some sugar. Another officer said "I've seen a lot of people with sugar diabetes that never acted like this. Ain't nothing wrong with the M.F. but drunk. Lock the S.B. up." ... Four officers grabbed Graham and threw him headfirst into the police car. ... Finally, Officer Connor received a report that Graham had done nothing wrong at the convenience store, and the officers drove him home and released him.
>
> At some point during his encounter with the police, Graham sustained a broken foot, cuts on his wrist, a bruised forehead, and an injured shoulder; he also claims to have developed a loud ringing in his right ear that continues to this day. He commenced this action under 42 U.S.C. 1983 against the individual officers in the incident, ... alleging that they had used excessive force in making the investigatory stop.

The Graham case raised an important legal question: When could an officer be sued civilly for excessive use of force? The Supreme Court ruled that a citizen can sue police for excessive use of force when the citizen's Fourth Amendment rights are violated. The Graham case is a seminal case for law enforcement officers and is covered in more detail in Chapter Five of this book. Here we are studying the Graham case and its relation to a legal test regarding *reasonableness*. With respect to that question, the Supreme Court ruled that

> [A]ll claims "that law enforcement officers have used excessive force-deadly or not-in the course of an arrest, investigatory stop, or other 'seizure' of a free citizen should be analyzed under the Fourth Amendment and its 'reasonable-ness' standard."... Determining whether the force used to effect a particular seizure is "reasonable" under the Fourth Amendment requires a careful bal-ancing of "the nature and quality of the intrusion on the individual's Fourth Amendment interest" against the countervailing governmental interests at stake. ... The "reasonableness" of a particular use of force must be judged from the perspective of a reasonable officer on the scene, rather than with the 20/20 vision of hindsight. ... The calculus of reasonableness must embody allowance for the fact that police officers are often forced to make split-second judgments-in circumstances that are tense, uncertain, and rapidly evolving- about the amount of force that is necessary in a particular situation ... **the "reasonable-ness" inquiry in an excessive force case is an objective one; the question is whether the officers' actions are "objectively reasonable" in light of the facts and circumstances confronting them,** without regard to their underlying intent or motivation. (emphasis added)[22]

So the Supreme Court recognized that the use of force by police is sit-uational, gave much deference to the circumstances faced by police, and held police accountable for their use of force, deadly or otherwise, through employment of an objectively reasonable standard. To put things clearly, police use of force, considering the circumstances, must be objectively reasonable.

Less Lethal Alternatives

Advances in technology are providing police officers with better less lethal options for use of force situations. In the past, officers had few options beyond a nightstick and their fists and grappling skills as less lethal alternatives at their disposal. Increasingly defensive tactics and martial arts skills are being incorporated into law enforcement training to increase the effectiveness of officers in physical force situations. The advent of new technologies has increased considerably the range of options that most officers have at their disposal in less lethal force situations. Those options have varying levels of success and the table below reflects data reported from a small study in 2005 on the effectiveness of Tasers and other options.

Less Lethal Weapon Effectiveness[23]

Weapon	Immediately Effective	Delayed Effectiveness	Not Effective	Total
TASER	191 (67.7%)	27 (9.6%)	64 (22.7%)	282 (100%)
Chemical agent	64 (83.1%)	4 (5.2%)	9 (11.7%)	77 (100%)
Impact weapon	8 (88.9%)	0 (0%)	1 (11.1%)	9 (100%)
Defense tactics	13 (54.2%)	4 (16.7%)	7 (29.1%)	24 (100%)
Bean bag	1 (100%)	0 (0%)	0 (0%)	1 (100%)
Total	277 (70.5%)	35 (8.9%)	81 (20.6%)	393 (100%)

It is important to note that "less lethal" weapons could in some circumstances still be lethal in effect and that they may not be effective or even appropriate in every situation. They are certainly much less likely to be lethal than firearms and when properly deployed in the correct situation, they may be very effective. We have provided below a brief overview of some of the basic types of less lethal options that are available to law enforcement. The largest issue with the increase in less lethal technologies in law enforcement is the lack of good empirical data on either the effectiveness or negative consequences of their use. Most data available come from the manufacturer of the devices in question rather than external research. That is beginning to change but until more data are available, the efficacy and dangers of these less lethal weapons will not be fully known.

While the number and types of less lethal options for law enforcement continue to increase as does their use and acceptance,[24] there is a certain level of resistance to them in many law enforcement agencies that arises from two important realities. The first and most important of those realities is that each addition to the range of possible options of an officer means that the officer will have to expend more time sorting between those options. To do that effectively, the officer will need additional and ongoing training at significant cost to the agency employing the officer. The second reality is that the presence of less lethal options at the scene of an incident gives rise to a perception in the mind of the public that less lethal options should be considered in every situation or that lethal force is no longer necessary,[25] justified, or perhaps even legal in some cases.[26] In reality, some situations such as a suspect pointing a weapon at an officer or others are not necessarily appropriate for exercising some less lethal options and it would be foolhardy to suggest that officers should always forego lethal force as a necessary first response. Even in such situations, the necessity of reasonableness and proportionality may require that officers consider other, less lethal options before resorting to lethal force in some cases even within the 21-foot rule.

KEY DEFINITION 17—21-FOOT RULE

A noncompliant individual within 21 feet of an officer can create an imminent danger to the officer. A hostile individual within 21 feet armed with a knife, blunt instrument, or even with fists can present an imminent danger as the hostile individual could close that 21-foot distance faster than an officer might be able to react.

Accordingly, an officer needs to be alert to the actions of people within 21 feet however they may be armed. Less lethal weapons are typically designed for use within this 21-foot zone to give officers an option other than the use of their firearm.

While the weapons listed below can be considered less lethal, they may result in lethal consequences even when used exactly as required. Officers need to be aware that at this point there are few, if any, truly nonlethal options available to them once the situation requires the application of physical force. So, even when using the types of devices listed below, it is important that officers consider the same issues of reasonableness and proportionality that apply to the application of more conventionally lethal force.

Conducted Energy Devices (Tasers)

Conducted energy devices are most commonly known by the more specific name Taser,[27] a specific type of device manufactured by Taser International that is currently the most commonly deployed variety of these devices. Tasers issued to law enforcement may have range up to 21 feet when the weapon is used with the "dart mode." That is, the Taser can fire a line with two electrodes up to 21 feet with relative accuracy. The darts ideally lodge in the individual and deliver a 50,000-volt shock, incapacitating the individual. Despite some recent concern over the safety of this weapon, the fact remains that it is much less lethal than a firearm and its use probably saves more lives than its nonuse would. In addition to the capacity to fire the electrode dart, some devices can be used as a stun gun as well without firing the electrode dart, a use with lower voltages and significantly fewer negative side effects. Only the individual receiving the direct effect of the Taser feels the electricity, and so officers can physically hold and subdue an individual while that individual is being given the shock.

There may be as many as 8,000 law enforcement agencies in the United States that have Taser devices, most commonly the TaserM26 or TaserX26, in service with their officers. The devices are widely touted as safe, less lethal alternatives to deadly force. Thus, they are frequently credited with reducing lethal force incidents across the United States. As the number of these devices has increased the controversy surrounding them has exploded. Questions about frequency of use,[28] use on people under the influence of drugs or alcohol, use on pregnant women, use on children, and easy availability of the devices to criminals are some of the issues that have been raised. These are not minor issues and several people nationally have died in close temporal proximity to exposure to Taser although the majority of those deaths have been attributed to drug use by the subject or to positional asphyxiation rather than to Taser deployment.

Though the use of Tasers remains controversial in some cases and in some jurisdictions, it is growing and it represents one of the safest less lethal alternatives available to law enforcement.[29] What is arguably needed is better articulation of national standards[30] for their use and increased levels of training[31] to ensure that officers understand and are able to comply with those standards in tactical situations.[32]

Chemical Sprays/Pepper Sprays/Aerosols

Pepper spray, also known as OC (*Oleoresin Capsicum*) is derived from peppers that affect the mucus membranes of humans and other animals. OC can be delivered in an aerosol or projectile form with either having significant results. Effects of OC often last for up to 45 minutes and can cause significant pain and incapacitation to those affected. OC spray is now a fixture in most law enforcement agencies and its use constitutes the largest category within physical use of force scenarios.[33]

OC appears to provide considerable advantages to law enforcement with few negative consequences. The spray significantly reduces physical aggressiveness; it is relatively short in duration and has a nearly 100% effectiveness rate; it works well on extremely agitated subjects or those under the influence of drugs or alcohol.[34] As with Taser technology, training is the key to the effectiveness of this less lethal alternative. However, when used properly, agencies have reported a reduction in officer and suspect injuries as well as a reduction in use of force or excessive force complaints.[35]

Other chemical sprays include agents such as CS gas, more commonly known as tear gas. This type of chemical spray is not normally part of a law enforcement officer's personally available options. These types of gasses are more commonly used in larger crowd control or riot control situation and their use normally requires additional training by officers.

Impact Weapons and Impact Projectiles

Wood batons are the most common form of impact weapon carried by law enforcement. In patrol or riot-lengths of 29" and 42" respectively, these weapons can cause serious injury and as with all force, must be used in a manner proportional to the threat. The larger, riot-length and weight batons are frequently issued to specialized units with law enforcement agencies and their use is often subject to additional training and control. Both these types of batons, as well as the aluminum PR-24 (ASP) telescoping baton, are intended in the first instance as a display of force not dissimilar to the uniform or the marked patrol car. The U.S. Department of Justice has recommended in the past that this type of display of force be included in investigations of use of force reports in the case of the Cincinnati Police Department.[36] The mere presence of a baton of wood or metal can often serve to induce compliance with no further force being necessary.

When display fails as an application of force, these batons are all intended to be used as impact weapons and to achieve compliance of the subject through the infliction of pain. If officers are not properly trained in their use, blows to some areas such as the head or groin can be severely debilitating and even lethal.[37] Use of other implements, such as metal flashlight as impact weapons has been increasing and this represents a dangerous development for law enforcement and has led to metal flashlight prohibitions in some jurisdictions.[38]

Bean bags fired from 12-gauge shotguns represent the second most common type of less lethal weapon deployed by law enforcement nationally. Additional types of less lethal projectiles including rubber bullets, OC pepperballs, and water cannons are other types of less lethal force sometimes employed by police. These projectiles have the advantage of allowing an officer to maintain significantly greater distance from the subjects. Most can be fired from a variety of weapons, many from the standard issue 12-gauge shotguns. Although these types of less lethal projectiles are useful in some situations, they are not normally part of an individual officer's readily available force alternatives. These options are generally exercised in crowd control or riot situations.

Crowd Control and Siege Situations

When a large number of officers respond to a situation in which they are confronted with a large number of subjects, the use of force has chaotic elements that cannot be controlled. All possible use of force incidents should be planned in advance as much as possible through the creation of in-depth policies and procedures, use of force continuum, and large-scale ongoing training of officers.

Crowd control and siege situations are specific, specialized, exceptionally difficult type of situations for law enforcement. These situations usually call for large numbers of officers to respond, often from several agencies. In many of these cases, the situations can be anticipated and planned in advance. It has been noted that in these types of situations, with large numbers of both subjects and responders, the paramilitary nature of some traditional police functions are heightened and intentionally brought to the fore. The reactions of officers in the event as well as afterward are similar in many cases to the reaction of individuals who have been in combat situations.[39]

In crowd control situations, law enforcement agencies act in ways very similar to military operations. Communication and coordination are crucial between units and between agencies. Individual actors as well as agencies must have clear standard operating procedures and clear lines of communication and command. Standard operating procedures also provide a basic framework and serve to condition and constrain thinking and decisional freedom, allowing officers to respond more quickly in emergency situations without having to completely reinvent the wheel every time they respond to a situation.

Standard operating procedures should lead to greater efficiency and better time management. The "op order" also known as an "Operations Order," is a useful element in siege situations or crowd control situations.[40] The operations order format can be modified to fit police and SWAT operations. Police do not necessarily deal with the "enemy," though in the post-9-11 world, they might. Generally police deal with citizens and suspects and the operations order should reflect this. Police should use an operations order format when planning large-scale or prolonged use of force engagements.

KEY DEFINITION 18—OPERATION ORDER

> The operations order is a standard format for organizing and planning police action and use of force. Operations orders may be issued for a variety of situations but are crucial whenever any law enforcement officer or agency responds to crowd control or siege incident.

Operation Order

Situation (describes current or anticipated circumstances)
    Perpetrators (numbers, identity, armed, intent, etc.)
    Friendly (other responding units—federal state, county, city, etc.;
    numbers)
    Civilian locations
Mission (goal of police operation)
Execution (how police will accomplish the goal)
    Rules of Engagement (how reasonable and proportional force is
    to be used—all need to be clear)
    Concept of operation (plan "A")[41]
        Maneuver
        Fire Support
        Obstacles
        NBC/Hazmat concerns
        Subunits mission
    Coordinating instructions
Service Support (prolonged operations will need logistic support:
food, water, ammo, replacement personnel, medical support, etc.)
Command and Signal (chain of command and lines of communication must be clear to all involved and easy to follow)

Use of the operations order format will standardize large unit response and make the police response more efficient and effective. In addition, police officers who have prior military experience will easily adapt to this method of planned response. The operations order should be updated and adapted to circumstances whenever necessary; the operations order depends on the situation entirely and should reflect current conditions as closely as possible. The operations order format would also work well in coordinating disaster response. Two other lessons can be learned from military training and adapted to police operations.

"Battle Drills" and "After Action Reviews," common military practice, can be very helpful to police. Police technically do not engage in "battles" but police are involved in "engagements." Therefore "Engagement Drills" can and should be conducted. For example, officers could specifically train to react to a sniper, a shooter, hazmat, or to other threats. Drills are important components of training as they allow officers to realistically simulate use of force necessary in various types of engagements and in reacting to them. Through drills they also come to better understand issues of reasonableness and proportionality; the officers' reactions also become faster and more efficient as well as more reasonable in responding to the real situation. The military, for example, uses drills extensively. F.A.T.S. (firearms training simulator) drills are in effect engagement drills of sorts, though officers should make the training as realistic as possible and enact the scenario as close to the real situation as possible.

KEY DEFINITION 19—ENGAGEMENT DRILL

> **An engagement drill is similar to a military battle drill. Officers practice responding to simulated scenarios to hone their reactions and refine their judgment.**

After Action Reviews should be standard operating procedure for all police departments and required at least whenever deadly force is used. After Action Reviews are conducted when reasonably feasible *on the scene immediately after* the situation is resolved. A spot is selected and the key officers and a supervisor assemble. The responsible officer explains, often with the use of sticks or rocks on the ground representing who was where and explaining what happened and discussing what went well and what did not. An After Action Review is a kind of forced reflection immediately after the situation is resolved. After Action Reviews are invaluable learning tools.

KEY DEFINITION 20—AFTER ACTION REVIEW

> **An After Action Review is an exercise of reflection immediately after the event. It is a critical analysis of what went right, what went wrong, what was not expected, and what the actors would do next time.**

Case Study:
Ruby Ridge—What Went Wrong?[42]

The siege at Ruby Ridge, Idaho, in 1992 was a siege situation that deteriorated quickly resulting in the deaths of Randy Weaver's son Sammy, his wife Vicki, and a federal marshal, William Degan. Kevin Harris was shot and wounded. In the Rugby Ridge siege the response of the subjects and law enforcement responses at the individual and administrative levels illustrate many of the issues surrounding use of force.

Randy Weaver was wanted on weapons charges and federal marshals went to Weaver's rural property to conduct surveillance. The Weavers' dog happened upon one of the agents and the agent shot the dog. Sammy Weaver investigated the dog's killing, and he and agent William Degan were both killed as a result of an encounter in the woods surrounding the cabin. The remaining individuals at the site retreated to the cabin and barricaded themselves in. Thus began the siege at Ruby Ridge.

The siege lasted about 11 days and received much national media coverage. The FBI and numerous law enforcement agencies responded to the situation. The Justice Department was under tremendous pressure to resolve the siege situation, and in an unusual and illegal move, modified the traditional rules of engagement and rules covering the use of deadly force. Traditional rules of engagement with deadly force allowed agents to fire when someone's life, either that of the officer or another individual, was in imminent danger. The modified rules of engagement allowed FBI agents to shoot on sight any adult seen with a weapon near the cabin. After that change, Lon Horiuchi, a FBI sniper, shot and killed Vicki Weaver as she stood behind the cabin door. The FBI would have a tough time explaining the shooting of Vicki Weaver based on the preexisting use of force guidelines for the agency.

> At Ruby Ridge, the Hostage Rescue Team ("HRT") was operating in accordance with rules of engagement that were reasonably subject to interpretation that would permit a violation of FBI policy and the Constitution. Those rules said that, under certain circumstances, certain persons "can and should" be the subject of deadly force. Those rules of engagement were contrary to law and FBI policy.[43]

Lon Horiuchi testified that he did not shoot pursuant to the modified rules of engagement[44] and other FBI agents testified before congressional hearings regarding the discussion of modified rules of engagement at Ruby Ridge: "My reaction is you've got to be kidding" agent Donald Kusulas told the committee. Agent Peter King said, "[T]that's crazy;

that's ridiculous," and both men testified that they decided not to follow rules of engagement that allowed them to shoot on sight any armed adult male.[45] It should be emphasized that the siege was a tense, dangerous, and fluid situation. Agents are regularly and well trained regarding the use of deadly force. Discussion of modified rules of engagement, or rules of engagement, in general, was a rarity and at best it injected confusion into an already tense situation. Agents Kusulas and King rightly stuck to their training and stood by their understanding of the proper use of deadly force, as did the vast majority of law enforcement officers involved—probably all agents did so. It is tough to know exactly what happened on that fateful day.

It is possible that FBI sharpshooter Lon Horiuchi was tracking a legitimate target that moved toward an object (the door) and fired at what he thought was a legitimate moving target and instead accidentally ended up striking and killing Vicki Weaver. Did Agent Horiuchi act in an objectively reasonable manner in firing two shots in the Ruby Ridge incident? It is probably the case, but that question is tough to answer and reasonable minds may differ on the answer. When it comes to questions regarding the employment of deadly force, it is not good when reasonable minds can and do differ regarding the appropriateness of use of force. Close calls, as in Ruby Ridge, will occur, though. The killing of Vicki Weaver did appear to be a tragic accident and the Ruby Ridge incident was a tragedy for all involved. One lesson for law enforcement to take away from the incident is to avoid siege situations if at all possible.[46] A second lesson for law enforcement to take away is that it is absolutely necessary that all involved be clear regarding the proper use of deadly force, and good communication is essential toward that end. Talk of rules of engagement and of changing rules of engagement is inappropriate and unnecessary as there is only one standard for use of deadly force.

In August 1995, the federal government settled a wrongful death suit by the Weaver family for more than three million dollars. The one standard rule regarding use of deadly force comes from an older case. The rule from the Supreme Court case of *Tennessee v. Garner* is clear and is applicable even in siege situations. "An officer can use deadly force only when he reasonably believes that his life or another's life is in danger, or if he reasonably believes that he or another faces grave bodily injury."

Case Study: World Series Crowd Control—What Went Wrong?

Victoria Snelgrove, a 21-year-old college student, was killed tragically, in Boston after the Red Sox beat the New York Yankees in a playoff series victory. Approximately 80,000 people spilled out of bars and their homes around Fenway Park after midnight and, "[a]s the crowd grew unruly, a police officer fired the pepper-spray weapon, striking 21-year-old Victoria Snelgrove, a college student, in the eye, which caused her death several hours later"[47] The pepper-spray weapon is designed as a less than lethal alternative to firearms, and usually is not fatal.

A pepperball weapon, or shotgun that fires bean bags instead of lead shot could be fatal if an individual is struck at extremely close range and possibly struck in the head. Ms. Snelgrove was tragically hit in the head with pepperball shot—the only question would be why?[48] Did the pepperball gun misfire (mechanical error), or, was human error to blame because the pepperball weapon was incorrectly employed? Police should consider using other means including water cannons, and mounted patrols to control crowds, as they may be less risky to employ in some circumstances. Officers using pepperball weapons should fire the weapon in such a manner as to not strike people above the torso if possible. Whatever the means employed, police need to train for the appropriate use of force and proper use of less lethal weapons.

Importance of Training/Certification

Since training for the use of deadly force is a serious matter, appropriate training must be provided by law enforcement. Some police departments maintain a firearms training simulator, known as F.A.T.S., which provides realistic video simulations of scenarios officers may encounter in real life, and helps officers hone their judgment on when to shoot and when not to shoot. F.A.T.S. training is very important and all police should undergo F.A.T.S. training, ideally on a regular basis. Live fire qualification with firearms is also crucial to ensure the officer's familiarity with the service weapon. There is no substitute for firing a real firearm and practicing with the firearm. Ideal firearms training would combine the regular use of F.A.T.S. and live fire qualification at the range. Police officers should be regularly trained and certified in the use of force.

Documenting Use of Force

"A picture is worth a thousand words." Though it is true that pictures and videos sometimes do not tell the whole story and can be taken out of context, they often provide excellent evidence of police encounters with civilians. Dash-mounted cameras in police cruisers are a fine example of a smart use of video technology to record traffic stops by police. Such recording helps protect both officers and citizens. As officers are using computers more and more, and digital cameras are becoming more capable and less expensive, it might make sense for officers to officially use digital cameras to record each response that they make, and then download that digital video to the computer in their squad car or headquarters for later review. A camera could be fitted into police helmets or hats, much like the dash-mounted video cameras; miniaturization of electronics will undoubtedly lead to such cameras in the future. Since more and more citizens have digital cameras; maybe officers should as well.

Hypotheticals

Less lethal means of apprehension such as chemical sprays, bean bags and rubber bullets, and Tasers alter the situation and reasonableness of response. In 1973 Officer Hymon of the *Tennesse v. Garner* case did not have a Taser or other effective less lethal means at his disposal. What if he had? What if he had a choice to use a less lethal means of apprehending the suspect and did not use it? Consider the facts of *Garner* and alter them for discussion purposes. What if Officer Hymon had a Taser and a firearm and thought, "huh, I have a firearm and a Taser and this guy is not armed, within Taser range, and I have probable cause to arrest for a felony, well, I will shoot him in the back of the head"? Officer Hymon would probably be arrested and face first degree murder charges. Under the circumstances, his use of force would not be reasonable, necessary, or proportional. Even under the actual facts, Officer Hymon's use of force did not appear proportional or reasonable. The use of Tasers is becoming common in law enforcement departments across the country as the Taser provides a reasonable and less lethal alternative to the use of firearms in many cases.

Questions for Discussion

Consider the following questions. How would you answer them?

1. In what ways is a use of force continuum useful for officers? In what ways is it problematic? How can these tools be made to be more effective?
2. What are the pros and cons of an officer carrying less lethal alternatives with him? Are the benefits worth the risks?
3. How important is the ability to apply physical force to a modern law enforcement officer? Given options other than "hands on control" techniques, should more emphasis be placed on other aspects of use of force in training?
4. What should the role of training be in the application of physical force? What should training provide to the officer and what can it *not* provide?

Chapter Three

Custodial Interrogation

What Is Custodial Interrogation?

The term "custodial interrogation" probably brings to most people's minds the image of a small dark room occupied by two detectives and an obviously guilty subject—exactly the image of "interrogations" that is portrayed in the media on countless nightly cop shows. In reality, custodial interrogation is much more nuanced and is a frequent duty of nearly every police or other law enforcement officer.

Before we examine custodial interrogation, we need to first examine what is meant by the term "custodial." Custody is understood to be a detention, which as discussed in Chapter One is a type of seizure. When an officer responds to an incident, it is not at all uncommon that he seizes a person or perhaps things. Recall the key definition of seizure from Chapter One:

KEY DEFINITION 2—SEIZURE

> Seizure is a broad concept including detentions, brief or lengthy, of property or people. The term implies the removal of something from the possession of another or removing the freedom of movement in the case of an individual

being seized. A law enforcement officer may briefly seize or detain an individual and may do so with less than probable cause for purposes of a brief investigation. Higher standards are required to make full arrests.

The person seized may become a suspect and the things seized may become evidence of a crime. Custody, the seizure of an individual, is nearly always undertaken to ascertain additional information and so it leads almost inevitably to interrogation, that is, questioning of some kind. As part of the process of determining what those people and things are and how they relate to the call to which he is responding, the officer often questions people, ultimately to find out whether a crime has been committed. Interrogation, if done legally, can properly aid in solving crimes and closing cases. If interrogations are done improperly, as with any improper application of force, the results can be damaging to the case, to the officer, and to the citizen.

It is important to develop a good understanding of what constitutes custody as a seizure and how seizures can be accomplished properly, because when an individual is seized in an explicitly custodial manner by police, constitutional rights attach. There are some exceptions; traffic stops as a very limited seizure, for instance. In general, however when an individual is seized and detained by law enforcement, other rights such as the constitutional rights that the Supreme Court enunciated in *Miranda v. Arizona*, for example, will come into play and these are discussed later in this chapter.

The concepts of "seizure," "custody," and "arrest" are quite intertwined. Both custody and arrest are seizures and the difference between the two terms is a matter of semantics and degree. Seizures may or may not be considered fully custodial, as in a Terry Stop, but an arrest is always considered fully custodial. When an officer seizes a person and that person does not feel able to leave the presence of the officer or to refuse the requests of the officer, that custodial seizure becomes an arrest. There are some Supreme Court precedents that help illustrate what constitutes a seizure or custody for purposes of custodial interrogation.

The first case, *Florida v. Bostick*,[1] is a case that sets a legal standard and definition for the term "arrest," a completely custodial state. As you read the fact pattern below, consider for yourself whether you believe that Mr. Bostick was arrested. Consider whether he was or could reasonably feel that he was free to leave or to not comply with the requests of the officers. Remembering that reasonableness is the basic standard for all uses of force, consider whether a *reasonable person* would consider Bostick to be arrested.

> Two officers, complete with badges, insignia and one of them holding a recognizable zipper pouch, containing a pistol, boarded a bus bound from Miami to Atlanta during a stopover in Fort Lauderdale. Eyeing the passengers, the officers admittedly without articulable suspicion, picked out the defendant passenger [Bostick] and asked to inspect his ticket and identification. The ticket, from Miami to Atlanta, matched the defendant's identification and both were immediately returned to him as unremarkable. However, the two police officers persisted and explained their presence as narcotics agents on the lookout for illegal drugs. In pursuit of that aim, they then requested the defendant's consent to search his luggage. Needless to say, there is a conflict in the evidence about whether the defendant consented to the search of the second bag in which the contraband was found and as to whether he was informed of his right to refuse to consent.[2]

Initially in the encounter, the police did not have a reasonable articulable suspicion sufficient to support even a Terry Stop of Bostick, nor did police have probable cause for a custodial seizure or arrest of Bostick. The question is whether the police "seized" Bostick and if they did, in doing so whether they violated his Fourth Amendment rights. If the answer is "yes," the seizure would be illegal and evidence seized as a result of the illegal seizure could be excluded by a court as "fruit of the poisonous tree." In *Florida v. Bostick*, the Supreme Court announced a rule to determine whether or not police had seized an individual in a manner consistent with arrest: "[T]he appropriate inquiry is whether a reasonable person would feel free to decline the officers' requests or otherwise terminate the encounter."

This then appears to create a relatively simple test to determine whether an individual was seized in a manner consistent with arrest, within the meaning of the Fourth Amendment. There are problems, however. The most obvious problem with this rule is that it does not exactly establish a bright-line rule that is easy to apply. In fact, the Supreme Court was split on how to apply that test to the facts of the

Bostick case. The majority, applying the test announced, concluded that a reasonable person in Bostick's position would indeed have felt free to decline the officers' requests or otherwise terminate the encounter. Three Justices dissented from that view, saying that the language of the test was fine, but, applying the rule to the facts of *Bostick* case, a reasonable person in Bostick's position would not feel free to decline the officers' request or otherwise terminate the encounter. Despite the problems in application, the working definition then of a seizure of a person or one who is in custody or one who is arrested for purposes of the Fourth Amendment remains that found in the *Bostick* case.

KEY DEFINITION 21—CUSTODY AND ARREST

"[T]he appropriate inquiry is whether a reasonable person would feel free to decline the officers' requests or otherwise terminate the encounter." "If the answer is 'no,' then the individual is in custody."[3]

Now that we have examined "custody," and we have a legal rule to determine when an individual is in custody, we need to turn our attention to questions of interrogation of an individual who is in custody. In custodial interrogation the most obvious place to begin is with an examination of the famous case of *Miranda v. Arizona*[4] and then to apply the holding in that case to other aspects of custodial interrogation. The Miranda rule is important because though controversial when first decided, it has become a well- known and important rule of criminal procedure law regarding custodial interrogation. Stated simply, the Miranda rule sets the parameters for custodial interrogation.

Confessions are and have always been prized by law enforcement. However, law enforcement before *Miranda* and some times since, went to really extraordinary lengths, some would say unconscionable lengths, to secure confessions. Confessions obtained through illegal coercion are of questionable value, and law enforcement should obtain confessions in a legally fair manner. In fact an effective, if not counterintuitive, method of interrogation is to be nice to the suspect![5] The Fourteenth Amendment's Due Process clause, Fifth Amendment's prohibition against self-incrimination and Due Process clause, and the Sixth Amendment's right to counsel in addition to the Fourth Amendment are implicated in situations of custodial interrogation.[6] The Miranda rule discussed in key definition 23 helps protect individual rights implicated by all of the above-mentioned areas of constitutional law. On occasion the Supreme Court will combine a number of cases that present similar issues into one large case, mainly to make a point of a sweeping precedent. The Supreme Court combined four separate cases concerning custodial interrogation into one large case in *Miranda*. Consider the basic facts of the cases that led to the Supreme Court's quite specific rule governing custodial interrogation in *Miranda*:

> In *Miranda v. Arizona*, the police arrested the defendant and took him to a special interrogation room where they secured a confession. In *Vignera v. New York*, the defendant made oral admissions to the police after the interrogation in the afternoon, and then signed an inculpatory statement upon being questioned by an assistant district attorney later the same evening. In *Westover v. United States*, the defendant was handed over to the Federal Bureau of Investigation by local authorities after they had detained and interrogated him for a lengthy period, both at night and the following morning. After some two hours of questioning, the federal officers had obtained signed statements from the defendant. Lastly, in *California v. Stewart*, the local police held the defendant five days in the station and interrogated him on nine separate occasions before they secured his inculpatory statement.[7]

Each of the above-mentioned fact patterns raises questions about proper police procedure in custodial interrogation. That is why the Supreme Court combined the cases into one big case. The Supreme Court announced one important new rule of constitutional law:[8]

> The prosecution may not use statements, whether exculpatory or inculpatory, stemming from custodial interrogation of the defendant unless it demonstrates the use of procedural safe guards effective to secure the privilege against self-incrimination. By custodial interrogation, we mean questioning initiated by law enforcement officers after a person has been taken into custody or otherwise deprived of his freedom of action in any significant way. As for the procedural safeguards to be employed, unless other fully effective means are devised to inform accused persons of their right of silence and to assure a continuous opportunity to exercise it, the following measures are required. *Prior to any questioning, the person must be warned that he has a right to remain silent, that any statement that he does make may be used as evidence against him, and that he has a right to the presence of an attorney, either retained or appointed. The*

defendant may waive effectuation of these rights, provided the waiver is made volun-
tarily, knowingly and intelligently. If, however, he indicates in any manner and at any
stage of the process that he wishes to consult with an attorney before speaking there
can be no questioning. Likewise, if the individual is alone and indicates in any
manner that he does not wish to be interrogated, the police may not question
him. The mere fact that he may have answered some questions or volunteered
some statements on his own does not deprive him of the right to refrain from
answering any further inquiries until he has consulted with an attorney and
thereafter consents to be questioned. (emphasis added)[9]

From this precedent comes the famous "Miranda warnings," which
are required prior to custodial interrogation. When *Miranda* was first
decided, it was quite unpopular and Congress passed a federal statute,
18 U.S.C. Section 3501 in an attempt to overturn the case. In the decades
that followed, the Supreme Court has attempted to clarify what its decision in *Miranda* means and when the requirements of *Miranda* apply.
In *Dickerson v. United States*[10] in 2000, the Supreme Court ruled defini-
tively that the Miranda warnings were indeed required, crucial, and not
superseded by 18 U.S.C. Section 3501. While that ruling may have not
had a significant impact on the way line officers approach the process of
custodial interrogations, it did cement completely the essential holding
of *Miranda* and make clear that the requirements of the basic Miranda
warning are here to stay in the American legal system.[11]

It should be noted that though the Constitution does not require
the prophylactic measure of the Miranda warning, the Supreme Court
does. A failure to provide the specifics of the Miranda warning outlined
above does not mean necessarily that a violation of the Fifth or Sixth
Amendment has taken place. In the absence of some unduly coercive
pressure, it may be that no violation of the individual rights exists. What
the Miranda warning does is provide a proactive notice to the individual
in custody and prevent the possibility that such a coercive atmosphere
might exist in the absence of the individual's knowledge of his rights.
Warning the suspect that he has a right to remain silent can only serve
to help protect his Fifth Amendment right against self-incrimination,
and the clause regarding the right to the presence of an attorney helps
protect and give meaning to the Sixth Amendment right to counsel.
Recall that the Miranda warnings require that once taken into custody,

an individual be informed that he has a right to counsel. That right to counsel, grounded in the Sixth Amendment, is an important right within the context of custodial interrogation. Note also in the italicized language above that if a suspect in custody indicates that he wishes to talk to an attorney before speaking, there can be no questioning.

KEY DEFINITION 22—RIGHT TO COUNSEL

If a suspect in custody indicates that he wishes to talk to an attorney before speaking, there can be no questioning.[12]

Officers need to be careful in dealing with a person whom they have in custody. There are some exceptions to the general rule the Supreme Court provided in *Miranda*, but they can get complex. It is, in almost every case, a better policy to err on the side of caution and not try to employ a technicality to justify custodial interrogation without a proper Miranda warning. Remember, if a confession is illegally obtained, potentially the confession and all evidence seized as a result of the illegally obtained confession could be excluded from all future proceedings and a guilty criminal could go free.

KEY DEFINITION 23—MIRANDA WARNING

Prior to any questioning, the person must be warned that he has a right to remain silent, that any statement that he does make may be used as evidence against him, and that he has a right to the presence of an attorney, either retained or appointed.

Police officers and all who study police use of force are aware of the Miranda warnings, as they are crucial to setting guidelines as to how custodial interrogation should proceed. Additionally, the Miranda warnings taken all together help to protect an individual's right to due process guaranteed by the Fifth and Fourteenth Amendments.[13]

Due Process

While *Miranda* and ultimately *Dickerson* provide the most definitive statements about rights that must be protected during custodial interrogations, cases that preceded *Miranda* are still relevant and illustrative. Two cases in particular further illustrate problems with tactics when carrying out custodial interrogations, and these cases were decided before *Miranda* and on legal grounds different from those of *Miranda*. The following two cases were decided on due process grounds, which can still be argued today, though the Supreme Court has moved away from due process analysis of custodial interrogation cases post *Miranda*. Just because the Supreme Court has not focused significantly on due process claims in custodial interrogation cases recently, it does not mean that they will not do so in the future. Fairness or due process claims can easily arise in cases of custodial interrogation.

KEY DEFINITION 24—DUE PROCESS

> Due Process is guaranteed by the Fifth and Fourteenth Amendments. Procedural due process requires notice, a hearing, and an opportunity to be heard. Substantive due process requires actual fairness in proceedings. Due process essentially requires fairness. Violation of due process can be argued when procedure or substance is not fair.

The terms "coercion" and "entice" often arise in discussions concerning custodial interrogation and their validity. Arguably all custodial interrogation is coercive, and some may involve enticement; sometimes the lines between the two can blur. Either unduly coercive interrogation tactics or excessive enticement in interrogation could potentially be illegal. Think of the carrot and stick approach; the carrot approach involves enticement and the stick approach is coercive. At some point coercion can become torture, and torture is a violation of due process, arguably a violation of the Fifth Amendment's privilege against self-incrimination, and a violation of the Eighth Amendment's prohibition against cruel and unusual punishment. President Bush's "War on Terror" and his administration's associated tactics at Camp X-Ray in Cuba and elsewhere have raised this exact question and problem. In fact, one of the military prosecutors at Guantanamo refused to prosecute an alleged terrorist "because he thought evidence was tainted by torture."[14]

Considering that the Colonel is a lifelong Marine and that he lost a close friend in the 9/11 terrorist attacks in New York, his concerns about the illegal use of torture to produce confessions and evidence should give one pause regarding the subject of custodial interrogation.[15] Custodial interrogation must not become unduly coercive in nature and must obviously not cross the line into torture. Custodial interrogation arguably did in some cases cross the line into what one would consider torture in Iraq in part because the guidelines on what was and was not permissible were not clear.[16] Not all coercive tactics need to be physical in nature. Actually *using* the stick is physically coercive and certainly excessive. Threatening to use the stick is psychologically coercive and no less problematic from the perspective of due process and the protection of rights. Excessive, undue psychological or physical coercion is prohibited by United States constitutional law as expounded by the Supreme Court in *Miranda* and elsewhere. Undue coercion always violates the right of an individual to due process.

Costs and Benefits

Consider the facts of the following case and ask yourself if these methods of interrogation described are unduly coercive. Remembering that the core standard in use of force is reasonableness, it is always prudent to ask whether a *reasonable person* would consider the interrogation tactics used below as unduly coercive.

> They took him to an office or room on the northwest corner of the fifth floor of the Shelby County jail. This office is equipped with all sorts of crime and detective devices such as fingerprint outfit, cameras, high-powered lights, and such other devices as might be found in a homicide investigating office. It appears that the officers placed Ashcraft at a table in this room on the fifth floor of the county jail with a light over his head and began to quiz him. They questioned him in relays until the following Monday morning, June 16, 1941, around nine-thirty or ten o'clock. It appears that Ashcraft from Saturday evening at seven o'clock until Monday morning at approximately nine-thirty never left this homicide room on the fifth floor.[17]

The facts of the Ashcraft case above sound as if they came from a bad old detective movie. And it seems plausible that any reasonable person would consider the above-mentioned facts unduly coercive.

The marathon relay questioning at the stationhouse is an example of how the state can use its advantage of controlling the time, place, and manner of the proceeding or interrogation and use the time, place, and manner of the interrogation in an unfair and unduly coercive way. The Supreme Court eventually reviewed the facts in Ashcroft and ruled in consistence with the reasonable person.

> We think a situation such as that shown here by uncontradicted evidence is so inherently coercive that its very existence is irreconcilable with the possession of mental freedom by a lone suspect against whom its full coercive force is brought to bear. It is inconceivable that any court of justice in the land, conducted as our courts are, open to the public, would permit prosecutors serving in relays to keep a defendant witness under continuous cross examination for thirty-six hours without rest or sleep in an effort to extract a "voluntary" confession. Nor can we, consistently with Constitutional due process of law, hold voluntary a confession where prosecutors do the same thing away from the restraining influences of a public trial in an open court room.[18]

Where the time, place, and process of interrogation are used by the state in an unduly coercive way to obtain exculpatory or inculpatory statements, those statements are obtained in violation of due process.[19] Regardless of the motivations of the officers involved, the guilt of the suspect, or the perceived necessity of the tactics, the statements are not permissible and they are most likely to result in an ultimately negative outcome for the case and probably for the officers involved also. An examination of a second key case in which the question of due process violations was raised will reveal this possibility. Again ask whether, given the following facts, a reasonable person would consider the behavior of the officers unduly coercive.

> On November 12, 1947, a Wednesday, petitioner [Watts] was arrested and held as the suspected perpetrator of an alleged criminal assault earlier in the day. Later the same day, in the vicinity of this occurrence, a woman as found dead under conditions suggesting murder in the course of an attempted criminal assault. Suspicion of murder quickly turned towards petitioner and the police began to question him. They took him from the county jail to State Police Headquarters, where he was questioned by officers in relays from about eleven thirty that night until sometime between 2:30 and 3 o'clock the following morning. The same procedure of persistent interrogation from about 5:30 in

the afternoon until about 3 o'clock the following morning, by a relay of six to eight officers, was pursued on Thursday the 13th, Friday the 14th, Saturday the 15th, Monday the 17th, Sunday was a day of rest from interrogation. About 3 o'clock on Tuesday morning, November 18, the petitioner made an incriminating statement after continuous questioning since 6 o'clock the preceding evening. The statement did not satisfy the prosecutor who had been called in and he then took petitioner in hand. Petitioner, questioned by an interrogator of twenty years' experience as a lawyer, judge and prosecutor, yielded a more incriminating document.[20]

The above facts of *Watts* are quite similar to those of *Ashcraft* and again illustrate the power advantage that the state has over the individual in manipulating the time, place, and manner of the interrogation to such an extent that an unduly coercive atmosphere is created. A reasonable person would probably agree that the facts in the *Watts* case constituted undue coercion, perhaps even torture. An unduly coerced confession cannot be trusted as there is a reasonable chance any suspect will eventually succumb to such tactics and say whatever is wanted just to end the coercion. More importantly, an unduly coerced confession is unfairly obtained and violates an individual's right to due process. The Supreme Court ruled accordingly in *Watts*: "To turn the detention of an accused into a process of wrenching from him evidence which could not be extorted in open court with all its safeguards, is so grave an abuse of the power of arrest as to offend the procedural standards of due process."[21]

Interrogation is typically understood as questioning of a suspect probably at a police station house or similar location and with law enforcement controlling the environment very carefully. But interrogation can occur without direct, express questioning. Consider the facts of a case following *Ashcraft, Watts,* and *Miranda* clarifying what constitutes "interrogation." Would a *reasonable person* say the exchange that follows constitute interrogation?

While en route to the central station, Patrolman Gleckman initiated a conversation with Patrolman McKenna concerning the missing shotgun. As Patrolman Gleckman later testified:

A. At this point, I was talking back and forth with Patrolman McKenna stating that I frequent this area while on patrol and [that because a school for handicapped children is located nearby,] there's a lot of handicapped children running around this area, and God forbid one of them might find a weapon with shells and they might hurt themselves.

Patrolman McKenna apparently shared his fellow officer's concern:

A. I more or less concurred with him [Gleckman] that it was a safety factor and then we should, you know, continue to search for the weapon and try to find it.

Respondent then interrupted the conversation, stating that he would show the officers where the gun was located. ... He replied that he understood his rights, but "wanted to get the gun out of the way because of the kids in the area in the school."[22]

The "discussion" between the officers appeared to be designed to play upon the suspect's conscience and elicit an incriminating response. As in *Ashcraft*, and *Watts*, the police in this case, *Rhode Island v. Innis*,[23] controlled the time, place, and manner of the atmosphere and manipulated the atmosphere to gain an incriminating response from the suspect despite never addressing him directly.

In each of these three cases, police had a relatively captive subject. Though a due process claim and argument were not explicitly made and did not serve as the basis of the decision in the case of *Innis*, it could have been, as the similarities between all three cases are striking. The Supreme Court can and does raise constitutional issues on its own from time to time. Though parties may not raise a due process claim, it is always possible that the Supreme Court might do so. In the *Innis* case, the Supreme Court stated a clear legal test to determine whether or not custodial interrogation occurred and used it to arrive at a somewhat startling conclusion.

[T]he Miranda safeguards come into play whenever a person in custody is subjected to either express questioning or its functional equivalent. That is to say, the term "interrogation" under Miranda refers not only to express questioning, but also to any words or actions on the part of police (other than those normally attendant to arrest and custody) that the police should know are reasonably likely to elicit an incriminating response from the suspect.[24]

The surprise is not the test to determine interrogation, as that seems quite clear. Rather the surprise is that the Court in applying that clear rule to the facts outlined above concluded that Innis was *not* interrogated. The test announced in *Rhode Island v. Innis* is a fine test, though reasonable minds can apparently apply the test to different fact patterns and come out with different answers. This case illustrates well the complexity of custodial interrogation and the controversy that can result. Despite the outcome of the *Innis* case, the rule enunciated makes it clear that interrogations can and do include more than just the marathon relay interrogations of Watts or Ashcroft.

KEY DEFINITION 25—INTERROGATION

"The term 'interrogation' under Miranda refers not only to express questioning, but also to any words or actions on the part of police (other than those normally attendant to arrest and custody) that the police should know are reasonably likely to elicit an incriminating response from the suspect."[25]

As with the exclusionary rule, there are numerous technicalities and exceptions to the Miranda warnings and what constitutes custodial interrogation.[26] The best practice, when possible, is to follow the Miranda rule outright in situations of custodial interrogation as defined by *Innis* to avoid the temptation of relying on some apparent technicality to obtain a confession and get the confession admitted into evidence.

Custodial Interrogation

Miranda v. Arizona, 384 U.S. 436 (1966) arose from four separate cases that the Supreme Court consolidated on appeal. In each of the four separate cases, a suspect was taken into custody, questioned in a police interrogation room in which the suspect was alone with the interrogators, and never informed of the constitutional right against self-incrimination.

Miranda held that any statement, whether inculpatory or exculpatory, obtained as the result of custodial interrogation could not be used against the suspect in a criminal trial. "Custodial interrogation" is defined in *Miranda* as "questioning initiated by law enforcement officers after a person has been taken into custody or otherwise deprived of his freedom of action in any significant way." All evidence obtained through custodial interrogation is suspect, and is subject to exclusion at trial unless the suspect has been notified of right against compulsory self-incrimination. This is usually accomplished through the prophylactic procedural safeguard of the now famous "Miranda Warning" which requires that a suspect be informed that he has the right to remain silent, and that anything he says will be used against him in court; he must also be clearly informed that he has the right to consult with a lawyer and to have the lawyer with him during interrogation, and that, if he is indigent, a lawyer will be appointed to represent him.

(continued)

Element	Definition	Cases	Exceptions
Custody	A person is deemed to be in custody if he is deprived of his freedom of action "in any significant way." "Custody" requires the existence of coercive conditions that would cause a reasonable person to believe, under all the circumstances surrounding the interrogation that he is not free to go.	*Miranda v. Arizona*, 384 US 436 (1966).	Brief detentions are generally not considered to be custodial. These brief detentions may include "Terry Stop" detentions or traffic stops (see *Berkemer v. McCarty*, 468 US 420 [1984]). Not all environments which are coercive are necessarily custodial. Even a police interrogation room, the situation at issue in *Miranda*, may not create a custodial environment based on the "totality of the circumstance" of the interrogation. If the suspect came into the station voluntarily, was informed that he was free to leave at any time, and that he was not under arrest, the requirements of *Miranda* for custodial interrogation may not apply. It is necessary that a "reasonable person" would believe that to be the case and that he was *actually* free to leave, however (see *Oregon v. Mathiason*, 429 US 492 [1971]; *California v. Beheler*, 463 US 1121 [1983]).
Interrogation	For purposes of determining the necessity of a Miranda warning, "interrogation" has been defined by the Supreme Court in *Rhode Island v. Innis*, 446 US 291 (1980), as occurring whenever a person in custody is subjected to "either express questioning or its functional equivalent."	*Miranda v. Arizona*, 384 U.S. 436 (1966); *Rhode Island v. Innis*, 446 US 291 (1980).	Actions or words of a law enforcement officer that he does not reasonably believe will elicit information are not considered interrogations under *Miranda* and *Innis*. "[S]ince the police surely cannot be held accountable for the unforeseeable results of their words or actions, the definition of interrogation can extend only to words or actions on the part of police officers that they *should have known* were reasonably likely to elicit an incriminating response."

Element	Definition	Cases	Exceptions
	"That is to say, the term 'interrogation' under Miranda refers not only to express questioning, but also to any words or actions on the part of the police (other than those normally attendant to arrest and custody) that the police should know are reasonably likely to elicit an incriminating response from the suspect."		The confession of the suspect in the Innis case was deemed by the Court to have not violated the safeguards under Miranda because the officers' comments were brief; the comments were not particularly evocative; there was no effort to engage the suspect in a conversation; the officers had no particular knowledge that the suspect would be susceptible to that type of appeal and; the suspect was not dis-oriented or visibly upset at the time the comments were made. Other types of questions may also fall outside of the Miranda warning requirements. Specifically as stated in Innis, questions normally attendant to arrest and custody do not require the warning to be given. These questions include routine questions such as name, address, date of birth, and other data necessary to complete an arrest or booking procedure (see Pennsylvania v. Muniz 496 US 582 [1990]).

Special Exceptions to Miranda

In some very specifically defined sets of circumstances, a Miranda warning may not be required prior to even custodial interrogation by law enforcement officers. These exceptions to the general requirement have been tailored by the Supreme Court to be narrowly defined and applied.

Waiver	A waiver by the suspect of his Fifth Amendment rights under Miranda may be allowable on the basis of the totality of the cir-cumstances, if the waiver of rights is made voluntarily, knowingly, and intelligently (see Colorado v. Connelly, 479 U.S. 157 [1986]). No waiver of the right can be assumed from the silence of a suspect following the warning or from a subsequent confession by the suspect (see North Carolina v. Butler, 441 U.S. 369 [1979]).
Undercover police	Miranda warnings are not required of undercover police officers. The Court has held that even though these may be "interrogations" while in "custody" they are allowable under Miranda (see Illinois v. Perkins, 496 U.S. 292 [1990]).

(continued)

Exigent circumstances	There exists a public safety exception to the general requirement of a Miranda warning. The exception allows officers to ask questions designed to address a specific and immediate public safety concern such as a loaded weapon that had been hidden in a public place. The questions must be narrowly focused on the specific exigent concern (see *New York v. Quarles*, 467 US 649 [1984]).
Routine booking questions	Although they may constitute custodial interrogation under the *Innis* standard, questions asked "for record-keeping purposes only," or to secure the "bio-graphical data necessary to complete booking or pretrial services," fall within a "routine booking question" exception which exempts them from the necessity of a Miranda warning (see *United States v. Horton*, 873 F.2d 180, 181 n.2 [8th Cir. 1989]).

These process-based protections from *Miranda* and other cases apply to everyone suspected of wrongdoing, including police officers. The Supreme Court examined a case of police interrogations of other officers in *Garrity v. New Jersey*.[27] In that case, police officers were accused of fixing traffic tickets in New Jersey. "Before being questioned, each appellant [officer] was warned (1) that anything he said might be used against him in any state criminal proceeding; (2) that he had the privilege to refuse to answer if the disclosure would tend to incriminate him; but (3) that if he refused to answer he would be subject to removal from office."

Were these warnings unduly coercive? Essentially the officers were told to answer questions or perhaps lose their jobs. The Court phrased the issue presented more broadly to apply to all employees, not just to law enforcement officers. "Our question is whether a State, contrary to the requirement of the Fourteenth Amendment, can use the threat of discharge to secure incriminatory evidence against an employee." This is a good question and it illustrates another possible form of coercion, namely, economic coercion requiring cooperation on the threat of your livelihood. The Supreme Court ruled that such coercion is unconstitutional. "[T]he protection of the individual under the Fourteenth Amendment against coerced statements prohibits use in subsequent criminal proceedings of statements obtained under threat of removal from office, and that it extends to all, whether they are policemen or other members of our body politic." According to the *Garrity* decision then, an employee or officer who is given the choice of talking or losing their job, can talk but the statements made under the threat of job loss cannot be used against the officer or employee in a criminal matter. A statement given under such circumstances has come to be known commonly as a "Garrity statement."

KEY DEFINITION 26—GARRITY STATEMENT

When an officer is forced to make a statement under the threat of possibly losing his job, the officer can make a statement but that statement cannot be used against him in a criminal matter.

Pretext Stops and Traffic Stops as Custodial Interrogation

Traffic stops have some of the hallmarks of custodial interrogation, as individuals and their vehicles are actually seized and the officer questions the driver and perhaps other occupants. When we apply the test laid out above to determine whether the individuals are in custody, the question whether a *reasonable person* would feel free to terminate or otherwise end the traffic stop and just drive off arises. The answer, for anyone who has ever been pulled over is, "of course not!" No doubt traffic stops are custodial in nature, but for public policy reasons and citing the brief nature of traffic stops, the Court says they are not custodial to the degree of arrest for constitutional purposes. The Supreme Court has essentially created a fiction just for traffic stops, saying that traffic stops are not custodial in nature, despite the test above. At least they are not the same things as full-blown arrests.

> The threat to officer safety from issuing a traffic citation, however, is a good deal less than in the case of a custodial arrest. In Robinson, we stated that a custodial arrest involves "danger to an officer" because of the extended exposure which follows the taking of a suspect into custody and transporting him to the police station. We recognized that "[t]he danger to police officer flows from the fact of the arrest, and its attendant proximity, stress, and uncertainty, and not from the grounds for arrest." *A routine traffic stop, on the other hand, is a relatively brief encounter and "is more analogous to a so-called 'Terry stop'. . . than to a formal arrest."* (Emphasis added)[28]

Traffic stops do not typically result in custodial arrest, but they can. Some jurisdictions allow officers to arrest people for traffic infractions[29] and sometimes officers develop probable cause for arrest during the traffic stop as well. At that point, the nature of the situation changes from a brief traffic stop to a more involved and arguably more dangerous situation of custodial arrest.

As noted, traffic stops by themselves have historically been treated differently from full-blown custodial arrests by the Court and they are crucial for police as traffic stops are frequently significant duties of officers. Moreover, because of the massive number of traffic stops made by police on a regular basis, they are subject to frequent scrutiny by the public. Allegations of misconduct or improper application of force during these stops can incite the public and the media and raise important questions. When can officers conduct traffic stops and what rules apply to traffic stops? The Fourth Amendment provides some legal foundation for traffic stops as it protects people in various places and circumstances from illegal searches.[30] The Fourth Amendment provides:

> The right of the people to be secure in their persons, houses, papers, and effects against unreasonable seizures and searches may not be violated; and a warrant may not issue except on probable cause, supported by oath or affirmation, particularly describing the place to be searched and the persons and things to be seized. (Fourth Amendment, U.S. Constitution)

One of the most controversial tactics used by law enforcement in the area of traffic stops are so called pretext stops. A pretext stop occurs when an officer does not have a reasonable articuable suspicion or probable cause for a traffic stop but perhaps does have a feeling that someone is up to no good, or when the officer has a morally improper reason, like racism, for the stop. Pretext stops rely primarily on an officer's subjective intentions. Consequently, pretext stops can be extremely hard to prove. Sometimes if a pattern of pretext stops develops, then it may be possible to prove civilly that the stops were pretextual and the officer's subjective intentions could be inferred from the pattern of actions. Pretext stops are quite controversial but most believe that an officer's improper subjective intentions or biases should invalidate a traffic stop. In fact, one might argue that a traffic stop by an officer based on improper subjective intentions or improper biases is unfair and it violates due process.

The Supreme Court did issue a controversial and clear rule regarding pretext stops.[31] Consider the facts of the *Whren* case that follows and ask yourself if the traffic stop was proper and legal.

> On the evening of June 10, 1993, plainclothes vice squad officers of the District of Columbia Metropolitan Police Department were patrolling a "high drug area" of the city in an unmarked car. Their suspicions were aroused when they passed a dark Pathfinder truck with temporary license plates and youthful occupants waiting at a stop sign, the driver looking down into the lap of the passenger at the right. The truck remained stopped at the intersection for what seemed an unusually long time–more than 20 seconds. When the police car executed a U turn in order to head back toward the truck, the Pathfinder turned suddenly to its right, without signaling, and sped off at an "unreasonable speed." The policeman followed, and in a short while overtook the Pathfinder when it stopped behind other traffic at a red light. They pulled up alongside, and Officer Ephriam Soto stepped out and approached the driver's door, identifying himself as a police officer and directing the driver, petitioner Brown, to put the vehicle in park. When Soto drew up to the driver's window, he immediately observed two large plastic bags of what appeared to be crack cocaine in petitioner Whren's hands. Petitioners were arrested, and quantities of several types of illegal drugs were retrieved from the vehicle.[32]

The United States Supreme Court considered the facts in *Whren* and found no constitutional violations resulting from the officers' actions. The Court squarely considered whether officers' subjective intentions should be considered in Fourth Amendment search and seizure analysis and held:

> Subjective intentions play no role in the ordinary, probable cause Fourth Amendment analysis. ... [T]here is no realistic alternative to the common law rule that probable cause justifies a search and seizure. ... [T]he officers had probable cause to believe that petitioners had violated the traffic code. That rendered the stop reasonable under the Fourth Amendment, the evidence they discovered admissible.[33]

Through this holding, the Court puts great emphasis on the probable cause for valid traffic stops, and it places very little weight on the officer's subjective intentions before the traffic stop. This view can be seen as turning a blind eye to the problem of pretext stops altogether. This apparent indifference to pretext stops is one reason the *Whren* decision is often criticized. A due process violation could be argued if the officer's subjective intentions before the traffic stop are proven to be egregious; however, proving the officer's subjective intentions is exceedingly difficult. The best way to determine one's subjective intentions is to listen to what one says. If an officer cites a legitimate reason for a traffic stop and secretly harbors malintentions and the officer does not give voice to those subjective intentions, it is practically impossible to prove that specific stops are pretextual.

KEY DEFINITION 27—ALLOWABLE TRAFFIC STOPS

Traffic stops made on the basis of probable cause are valid allowable stops, regardless of the officer's subjective intentions. These stops represent temporary seizures of the vehicle and its occupants but are not considered custodial interrogations under the current law.

This rule, though somewhat controversial, is logical, easy to understand for judges, lawyers and lay people, and is a natural outgrowth of the Carroll doctrine regarding vehicles. Automobiles, unlike homes, have traditionally been afforded minimal Fourth Amendment privacy guarantees largely because of their inherent mobility. The brief background on the "automobile exception" that follows is important as traffic stops constitute a significant portion of a police officer's duties.

The United States Supreme Court first established the "automobile exception" regarding warrants and discussed probable cause regarding the stop of an automobile in a prohibition era case, *United States v. Carroll*. Consider the following facts:

Caroll smuggled alcohol during the prohibition era. Chief prohibition officer Cronenwett, acting undercover, made an agreement to purchase contraband whiskey from Carroll and two others on September 29, 1921. Cronenwett obtained a description of their car and its license plate number. The Carroll boys never delivered the alcohol. On December 15, Cronenwett and two other officers passed a car traveling in the other direction. Cronenwett recognized them and said, "There goes the Carroll brothers." The Officers turned around and pulled over and stopped Carroll's vehicle. The officers searched the vehicle without a warrant or consent and discovered two bottles of liquor.

Carroll admitted that they had six cases of liquor in the car. The officers confiscated the alcohol and took the defendants to jail.

Could the officers seize Carroll and search the car without a warrant, if officers did have probable cause to believe the Carroll brothers were illegally transporting contraband? Taking into consideration the undercover work of police described in the fact pattern above, it looked as if the officers had good reason, more correctly probable cause, for the traffic stop. The Supreme Court held in *Carroll*:

> [W]e have made a somewhat extended reference to these statutes to show that the guaranty of freedom from unreasonable searches and seizures by the Fourth Amendment has been construed, practically since the beginning of the government, as recognizing a necessary difference between a search of a store, dwelling house, or other structure in respect of a which a proper official warrant readily may be obtained and a search of a ship, motor boat, wagon, or automobile for contraband goods, where it is not practicable to secure a warrant, because the vehicle can be quickly moved out of the locality or jurisdiction in which the warrant must be sought.

The vehicle's mobility creates an exigent circumstance that allows officers to search the vehicle without a warrant, if the stop and search is based on probable cause.

KEY DEFINITION 28—READY MOBILITY OF VEHICLE

Ready mobility of a vehicle creates an exigent circumstance which allows officers to search a vehicle without a warrant, if officers have probable cause for the traffic stop and if officers have probable cause to believe the object of their search will be found in the automobile.

Traffic stops are an officer's best friend. Officers often do not need to get a search warrant to search cars as a result of the Carroll doctrine as discussed above. Considering the Court's clear ruling in *Whren*, that an officer's subjective intentions essentially do not matter in traffic stops, the fact that it is typically easy to establish probable cause for a traffic stop, and that traffic stops often lead to discovery of probable cause of other crimes, police departments may want to make regular use of enforcement of traffic codes. In some jurisdictions in which it is allowable to arrest an individual for a traffic violation, searches incident to arrest are justified.[34] In practice, and officer's subjective intentions for traffic stops are tough to prove. A department's and officer's ethics in conducting traffic stops are of paramount importance. Officers and police departments need to guard against overzealous enforcement of the traffic codes however, and actual or perceived pretextual stops based on racial or other improper motives can cause tremendous public relations problems and possibly result in unwanted legal challenges. Traffic stops can turn into situations of custodial arrest. Therefore officers need to remember that Miranda rights should be read to suspects who are arrested before they are interrogated or officers risk having the suspect's statements thrown out in court later. Custodial interrogation is a regular duty of police officers and if that is legally and properly carried out, it can aid law enforcement in fighting crime. If it is carried out in an illegal manner, then the evidence obtained from the confession and the confession itself may be thrown out and guilty criminals may go free. Those officers and departments that break the law may also face civil and or criminal liability. Liability of officers is the subject of the next chapter, Chapter Four.

To summarize, seizure, arrest, and interrogation, all go hand in hand. Law enforcement officers and those who study police use of force need to have a good grasp of those concepts. As demonstrated in this chapter, the Supreme Court has decided a number of precedents that give us legal tests and guidance regarding classifying seizures, arrests, and interrogations. For public policy reasons, the Supreme Court has created different degrees and categories of custody, without necessarily calling seizures custodial. More clearly, Terry Stops and traffic stops, while custodial in nature, are not typically considered as arrests—the most serious form of seizure (aside from actual imprisonment or execution); the Court created a lesser subcategory of seizures with its handling of Terry Stops and traffic stops. Officers need to be careful as these lesser custodial situations can easily and quickly escalate into unquestionably custodial arrest situations. As traffic stops are a significant duty of law enforcement officers, police should always keep in mind that question of reasonableness: would a reasonable person consider themselves free to leave? And time is always of the essence. The longer the duration of a traffic stop, the more likely it is to turn into a full-blown arrest. Gray areas of law often work against law enforcement, and so officers should do their best to respond clearly and reasonably to situations such as traffic stops. If an officer's motives for a detention or traffic stop are seen by the community as improper, members of the community will label the stop as a pretext stop. Law enforcement officers should consider the legality of their procedures as well as the community's perception of their procedures and do their best to keep both in sync in a positive way. They should strive to act in an objectively reasonable manner.

All custodial situations, if not all interaction between police and citizens, involve interrogation by police. Police necessarily ask questions of citizens. Problems can arise, however, when police take an individual or individuals into custody and then interrogate them, because remember, many constitutional rights attach after a person has been deemed to have been taken into custody. How custodial interrogation is handled by law enforcement can make or break a case, and can make or break relations with the community.

Questions for Discussion

Consider the following questions. How would you answer them?

1. How much coercion is acceptable in interrogation? What factors influence your answer?
2. Is there a legitimate role for profiling or pretext stops in law enforcement? What types of pretexts, if any, should be allowed or utilized and why?
3. What is a fair method of interrogation? What methods might be persuasive but not coercive as such?
4. Who should determine what practices are allowed and which are prohibited? What should the role of civilian and legislative oversight be in these matters?
5. What is the proper balance between the rights of the individual to be free from coercion and the necessity of the state to protect itself from criminals?

Chapter Four

Liability of Law Enforcement Officers

Abuse of power in the form of excessive use of force by police officers can lead to criminal and or civil legal liability. Department and individual ethics, culture, and oversight, or checks on abuse of power play a role in preventing abuse of power by law enforcement officers. If one follows the issue of use of excessive force by police officers over a long period of time, one will find that such allegations are almost commonplace, with allegations accruing on various scales in jurisdictions throughout the United States. It is enlightening to study some specific cases to determine how the abuse of power was detected and handled and what liability attached. Before looking at one of the most infamous incidents of use of excessive force by police, the Los Angeles Rampart scandal, it is helpful to discuss certain legal concepts and rules as established by the Supreme Court. Doing so will help to establish a framework and context within which to discuss excessive use of force by police and how best police officers may avoid excessive use of force charges. It is absolutely clear that excessive use of force by police is wrong; it should not occur and should be prevented. If excessive use of force by police does in fact occur, such bad conduct should be held accountable under criminal or civil law, or perhaps both.

Law enforcement officers are responsible to maintain law and order and to keep society and citizens safe. Toward that end sometimes police must use force against citizens. If one civilian hits another civilian with his fist, the offender has probably committed assault or battery and could be so charged, because the civilian has no special privilege (assuming self-defense is not applicable) and has no immunity from the laws against using force against another civilian. This immunity in particular is a key concept. Law enforcement officers enjoy immunity from essentially criminal laws if their actions, namely their uses of force, are reasonable and necessary to protect other individuals, other officers, themselves, or society as a whole. It would be impossible for police to do their jobs without some form of qualified immunity.

KEY DEFINITION 29—IMMUNITY OF LAW ENFORCEMENT OFFICERS

Law enforcement officers enjoy qualified immunity from laws regarding use of force, if that use of force is reasonable, necessary, and appropriate and in the course of executing official duties. Qualified immunity is thus a shield for law enforcement officers, but the shield is not absolute; excessive force is not shielded.[1]

Civil Liability

In cases of excessive use of force by police, the defense of qualified immunity of the officer or police department must be defeated if a legal action is to proceed. Civil suits are common[2] and the most typical action is a suit in federal court pursuant to Title 42 of the United States Code Section 1983. This statute provides the following:

Every person who, under color of any statute, ordinance, regulation, custom, or usage, of any State or Territory or the District or Columbia, subjects, or causes to be subjected, any citizen of the United States or other person within the jurisdiction thereof to the deprivation of any rights, privileges, or immunities secured by the Constitution and laws, shall be liable to the party injured in an action at law, suit in equity, or other proper proceeding for redress.[3]

These claims are know as "1983 actions."[4] In a 1983 action the plaintiff alleges that the government denied the plaintiff's civil rights in some fashion. A plaintiff in a 1983 action must prove two elements: "(1) that the plaintiff was deprived of a right secured by the Constitution or laws of the United States; and (2) that the deprivation was committed by a person acting under the color of state law."[5] It is helpful to examine an important precedent regarding 1983 actions.[6] In this case, Ms. Harris was arrested and transported to the police station.

> When she arrived at the station, Mrs. Harris was found sitting on the floor of the wagon. She was asked if she needed medical attention, and responded with an incoherent remark. After she was brought inside the station for processing, Mrs. Harris slumped to the floor on two occasions. Eventually, the police officers left Mrs. Harris lying on the floor to prevent her from falling again. No medical attention was ever summoned for Mrs. Harris. After about an hour, Mrs. Harris was released from custody and taken by ambulance (provided by her family) to a nearby hospital. There, Mrs. Harris was diagnosed as suffering from severe emotional ailments; she was hospitalized for one week and received subsequent outpatient treatment for an additional year.
>
> Sometime later, Mrs. Harris commenced this action alleging many state-law and constitutional claims against the City of Canton and its officials. Among these claims was one seeking to hold the city liable under 42 U.S.C. 1983 for its violation of Mrs. Harris's right under the Due Process Clause of the Fourteenth Amendment, to receive necessary medical attention while in police custody.[7]

Essentially the Supreme Court had to decide whether Mrs. Harris's 1983 action against the city alleging a failure to obtain medical attention could proceed. The Court attached significant weight to governmental policies and customs. "'It is only when the execution of the government's policy or custom … inflicts the injury' that the municipality may be held liable under 1983."[8] Was it the official policy or custom of the City of Canton to deny appropriate medical attention to those whom its officers had arrested? Did lack of training by the police department constitute a deprivation of Mrs. Harris's rights? Could Mrs. Harris proceed with such allegations in her 1983 lawsuit? The answer to the last question is "yes." She could proceed with her 1983 action and it would be up to a finder of fact in a court of law to determine the answers to the other questions above.

Specifically the Supreme Court ruled, "We hold today that the inadequacy of police training may serve as the basis for 1983 liability only where failure to train amounts to deliberate indifference to the rights of persons with whom the police come into contact."[9] Note that the Court used the term "deliberate indifference" as the standard of misconduct that the plaintiff would have to prove in a 1983 action. The burden on the plaintiff is pretty high, as it could be a challenge to show that a city's police department acted with deliberate indifference. It is not an impossible burden for a plaintiff to meet, however, and ultimately would be a question of fact for a court to resolve. A main point to take away from the *Canton v. Harris* case is that a plaintiff can file a civil 1983 lawsuit alleging that a police department's lack of training constituted a policy that led to a deprivation of the plaintiff's constitutional rights.

KEY DEFINITION 30—1983 ACTION

> **A 1983 action is a federal civil suit which alleges that an officer, police department, or governmental agency wrongfully violated the plaintiff's constitutional rights.**

A seminal Section 1983 case for law enforcement is the *Graham v. Connor* case.[10] We discussed this case previously in Chapter Three when discussing excessive use of force by police and specifically we discussed the Graham factors. As *Graham* is also a Section 1983 case, it merits further discussion and emphasis at this point. Consider the facts that follow: the court considered the evidence in a light that most favors the petitioner, a typical standard of review.

> On November 12, 1984, Graham, a diabetic, felt the onset of an insulin reaction. He asked a friend, William Berry, to drive him to a nearby convenience store so he could purchase some orange juice to counteract the reaction. Berry agreed, but when Graham entered the store, he saw a number of people ahead of him in the checkout line. Concerned about the delay, he hurried out of the store and asked Berry to drive him to a friend's house instead.
>
> Respondent Connor, an officer of the Charlotte, North Carolina Police, saw Graham hastily enter and leave the store. The officer became suspicious that something was amiss and followed Berry's car. About one-half mile from the store, he made an investigative stop. Although Berry told Connor that Graham was simply suffering from a "sugar reaction," the officer ordered Berry and Graham to wait while he found out what, if anything, had happened at the convenience store. When Officer Connor returned to his patrol car to call for back up assistance, Graham got out of the car, ran around it twice, and finally sat down on the curb, where he passed out briefly.

In the ensuing confusion, a number of other Charlotte police officers arrived on the scene in response to Officer Connor's request for backup. One of the officers rolled Graham over on the sidewalk and cuffed his hands tightly behind his back, ignoring Berry's pleas to get him some sugar. Another officer said: "I've seen a lot of people with sugar diabetes that never acted like this. Ain't nothing wrong with the M.F. but drunk. Lock the S.B. up." App. 42. Several officers then lifted Graham up from behind, carried him over to Berry's car, and placed him face down on its hood. Regaining consciousness, Graham asked officers to check in his wallet for a diabetic decal that he carried. In response, one of the officers told him to "shut up" and shoved his face down against the hood of the car. Four officers grabbed Graham and threw him head-first into the police car. A friend of Graham's brought some orange juice to the car, but the officers refused to let him have it. Finally, Officer Connor received a report that Graham had done nothing wrong at the convenience store, and the officers drove him home and released him.

At some point during the encounter with the police, Graham sustained a broken foot, cuts on his wrists, a bruised forehead, and an injured shoulder; he also claims to have developed a loud ringing in his right ear that continues to this day. He commenced this action under 42 U.S.C. 1983 against the individual officers involved in the incident, all of whom are respondents here, alleging that they had used excessive force in making the investigatory stop, in violation of "rights secured to him under the Fourteenth Amendment to the United States Constitution and 42 U.S.C. 1983."[11]

Factually there are similarities between the *Graham* case and the *Canton* case in that both cases involved individuals with acute medical problems being taken into custody. And both plaintiffs brought 1983 actions. There is an important distinction between the two however. In the *Canton* case, the plaintiff essentially alleged that the policy of the police department amounted to a denial of appropriate and necessary medical care, thus depriving the plaintiff of her constitutional rights. Harris did not challenge the amount of force used. Graham did challenge the amount of force used by police to detain him. Graham argued that the amount of force used by police was excessive and it caused him physical injuries, depriving him of his constitutional rights. The *Canton* case shows that plaintiffs can assert fairly broad policy allegations in a 1983 action and the *Graham* case specifically addresses allegations of excessive use of force by police. Moreover, the Supreme Court used the *Graham* case as a vehicle to send a message and set a precedent regarding how allegations of excessive use of force by police in 1983 actions should be evaluated under the law. The Supreme Court said:

> [W]e ... hold that *all claims that law enforcement officers have used excessive force-deadly or not in the course of an arrest, investigatory stop, or other "seizure" of a free citizen should be analyzed under the Fourth Amendment and its "reasonableness" standard*, rather than under a "substantive due process" approach. ...Determining whether the force used to effect a particular seizure is "reasonable" under the Fourth Amendment requires careful balancing of "the nature and quality of the intrusion on the individual's Fourth Amendment interests" against the countervailing governmental interest at stake. ... *The "reasonableness" of a particular use of force must be judged from the perspective of a reasonable officer on the scene*, rather than with the 20/20 vision of hindsight. (emphasis added)[12]

So an allegation of excessive use of force by police in a 1983 action should be judged for its reasonableness under the Fourth Amendment from a perspective of a reasonable officer on the scene, and as mentioned earlier in the book, the Graham factors can be so employed. Recall the Graham factors below:

KEY DEFINITION 31—GRAHAM FACTORS IN USE OF FORCE

One must examine the facts and the circumstances including

1. **The severity of the crime,**
2. **Whether the suspect posed an immediate threat to the safety of officers or others,**
3. **Whether the suspect is actively resisting, and**
4. **Whether the suspect is attempting to evade arrest by flight.**

It is also crucial to keep the statute of limitations in mind. Statutes of limitation exist in all civil and criminal legal actions except murder. If a legal action is not commenced within a set time frame, commonly two to four years in the case of a civil tort action, then the legal action is forever barred. The expiration of the statute of limitations can be a complete defense to a legal action. Potential plaintiffs and potential defendants must be aware of the statute of limitations. It is like the game clock in a sense; out of time is out of time. The statue of limitations applies in 1983 actions.[13]

KEY DEFINITION 32—STATUTE OF LIMITATIONS

A statute of limitations is a time period that, once expired, prevents further legal action from being brought. There is a civil and criminal statute of limitations for all legal actions except murder. The statute of limitations in a civil tort case is typically between two and four years. One must be aware of the statute of limitations; its expiration is an absolute bar to legal action and it is a common and successful defense to legal actions.

Remember that we discussed the concept of immunity and qualified immunity earlier in this chapter. The issue of qualified immunity must be addressed in excessive use of force cases. Consider the following fact pattern:

In autumn of 1994, the Presidio Army Base in San Francisco was the site of an event to celebrate conversion of the base to a national park. Among the speakers was Vice President Albert Gore, Jr., who attracted several hundred observers from the military and general public. Some in attendance were not on hand to celebrate, however. Respondent Elliot Katz was concerned that the Army's Letterman Hospital would be used for conducting experiments on animals. (Katz was president of a group called In Defense of Animals. Although both he and the group are respondents here, the issues we discuss center upon Katz, and we refer to him as "respondent"). To voice opposition to the possibility that the hospital might be used for experiments, respondent brought with him a cloth banner, approximately 4 by 3 feet, that read "Please Keep Animal Torture Out of Our National Parks." In the past, as respondent was aware, members of the public had been asked to leave the military base when they engaged in certain activities, such as distributing handbills; and he kept the banner concealed under his jacket as he walked through the base.

The area designated for the speakers contained seating for the general public, separated from the stage by a waist-high fence. Respondent sat in the front row of the public seating area. At about the time Vice President Gore began speaking, respondent removed the banner from his jacket, started to unfold it, and walked toward the fence and speakers' platform.

Petitioner Donald Saucier is a military police officer who was on duty that day. He had been warned by his superiors of the possibility of demonstrations, and respondent had been identified as a potential protestor. Petitioner and Sergeant Steven Parker—also a military police officer, but not a party to the suit—recognized respondent and moved to intercept him as he walked toward the fence. As he reached the barrier and began placing the banner on the other side, the officers grabbed respondent from behind, took the banner, and rushed him out of the area. Each officer had one of respondent's arms, half-walking, half-dragging him, with his feet "barely touching the ground." App.24. Respondent was wearing a visible, knee-high leg brace, although petitioner later testified he did not remember noticing it at the time. Saucier and Parker took respondent to a nearby military van, where, respondent claims, he was shoved or thrown inside. Id., at 25. The reason for the shove remains unclear. It seems agreed that respondent placed his feet somewhere on the outside of the van, perhaps on the bumper, but there is a dispute whether he did so to resist. As a result of the shove, respondent claims, he fell to the floor of the van, where he caught himself just in time to avoid any injury. The officers drove respondent to a military police station, held him for a brief time, and then released him. Though the details are not clear, it appears that at least one other protestor was also placed in the van and detained for a brief time. Id., at 27.

Respondent brought this action in the United States district Court for the Northern District of California against petitioner and other officials pursuant to *Bivens v. Six Unknown Fed.* Narcotics Agents, 403 US 388 (1971), alleging, inter alia, that defendants had violated respondent's Fourth Amendment rights by using excessive force to arrest him. (emphasis added)[14]

The Supreme Court set an important precedent regarding qualified immunity and excessive use of force cases. Qualified immunity legal analysis has steps and layers, a sort of decision tree. The Supreme Court ruled regarding the first step of the analysis:

A court required to rule upon the qualified immunity issue must consider, then, this threshold question: Taken in the light most favorable to the party asserting the injury, do the facts alleged show the officer's conduct violated a constitutional right? ... *If no constitutional right would have been violated were the allegations established, there is no necessity for further inquiries concerning qualified immunity.* (emphasis added)[15]

This first step of analysis appears to be clear. If there is no constitutional violation shown by the aggrieved party, then the case should be dismissed. But what if the plaintiff's allegations, if proved to be true, could constitute a violation of the Constitution? The Supreme Court, in that instance, ruled that

if a violation could be made out on a favorable view of the parties submissions, the next, sequential step is to ask whether the right was clearly established. ... "The contours of the right must be sufficiently clear that a reasonable official would understand that what he is doing violates that right." ... The relevant, dispositive inquiry in determining whether a right is clearly established is whether it would be clear to a reasonable officer that his conduct was unlawful in the situation he confronted. ... *If the law did not put the officer on notice that his conduct would be clearly unlawful, summary judgment based on qualified immunity is appropriate.* See *Malley v. Briggs*, 475 US 335, 341 (1986) (qualified immunity protects "all but the plainly incompetent or those who knowingly violate the law").[16]

So a reasonable officer would have to know that he is violating the law for liability to attach and qualified immunity to be defeated. What if the officer acted mistakenly?

If an officer reasonably, but mistakenly, believed that a suspect was likely to fight back, for instance, the officer would be justified in using more force than in fact was needed. ... The qualified immunity inquiry, on the other hand, has a further dimension. ... [E]ven if a court were to hold that the officer violated the Fourth Amendment by conducting an unreasonable, warrantless search, Anderson still operates to grant officers immunity for reasonable mistakes as to the legality of their actions. The same analysis is applicable in excessive force cases, where in addition to the deference officers receive on the underlying constitutional claim, *qualified immunity can apply in the event the mistaken belief was reasonable.*[17]

This gets interesting as, if an officer acts reasonably though mistakenly, qualified immunity still could apply if the officer made a reasonable mistake. A reasonable mistake may be excused though the court may have found a violation of the Fourth Amendment's prohibition against unreasonable searches and that principle applies in excessive use of force cases (see the quote above). The important point to remember here is that an officer who reasonably, though mistakenly, uses excessive force should be entitled to a defense of qualified immunity.

The Court in this case ruled that the officer did not knowingly and clearly violate any of Saucier's constitutional rights and the officer was entitled to qualified immunity.[18] The Supreme Court applied the qualified immunity analysis set out in *Saucier* in this next case. Consider the facts below:

On the day before the fracas, Glen Tamburello went to the police station and reported to Brosseau that Haugen, a former crime partner of his, had stolen tools from his shop. Brosseau later learned that there was a felony no-bail warrant out for Haugen's arrest on drug and other offenses. The next morning, Haugen was spray-painting his Jeep Cherokee in his mother's driveway. Tamburello learned of Haugen's whereabouts, and he and cohort Matt Atwood drove a pickup truck to Haugen's mother's house to pay Haugen a visit. A fight ensued, which was witnessed by a neighbor who called 911.

Brosseau heard a report that the men fighting in Haugen's mother's yard and responded. When she arrived, Tamburello and Atwood were attempting to get Haugen into Tamburello's pickup. Brosseau's arrival created a distraction, which provided Haugen the opportunity to get away. Haugen ran through his mother's yard and hid in the neighborhood. Brosseau requested assistance, and, shortly thereafter, two officers arrived with a K-9 to help track Haugen down. During the search, which lasted about 30 to 45 minutes, officers instructed Tamburello and Atwood to remain in Tamburello's pickup. They instructed Deanna Nocera, Haugen's girlfriend who was also present with her 3-year-old daughter, to remain in her small car with her daughter. Tamburello's pickup was parked in the street in front of the driveway; Nocera's small car was parked in the driveway in front of and facing the Jeep; and the Jeep was parked about 4 feet away from Nocera's car and 20 to 30 feet away from Tamburello's pickup.

An officer radioed from down the street that a neighbor had seen a man in her backyard. Brosseau ran in that direction, and Haugen appeared. He ran past the front of his mother's house then turned and ran into the driveway. With Brosseau still in pursuit, he jumped into the driver's side of the Jeep and closed and locked the door. Brosseau believed that he was running to the Jeep to retrieve a weapon.

Brosseau arrived at the Jeep, pointed her gun at Haugen, and ordered him to get out of the vehicle. Haugen ignored her command and continued to look for the keys so he could get the Jeep started. Brosseau repeated her commands and hit the driver's side window several times with her handgun, which failed to deter Haugen. On the third or fourth try, the window shattered. Brosseau unsuccessfully attempted to grab the keys and struck Haugen on the head with the barrel and butt of her gun. Haugen, still undeterred, succeeded in starting the Jeep. As the Jeep started or shortly after it began to move, Brosseau jumped back and to the left. She fired one shot through the rear driver's side window at a forward angle, hitting Haugen in the back. She later explained that she shot Haugen because she was "fearful for the other officers on foot who [she] believed were in the immediate area, [and] for the occupied vehicles in [Haugen's] path and for any citizens who might be in the area." 339 F. 3d, at 865.

Despite being hit, Haugen, in his words, "stood on the gas"; navigated the "small, tight space" to avoid other vehicles; swerved across the neighbor's lawn; and continued down the street. Ibid., at 882. After about a half a block, Haugen realized that he had been shot and brought the Jeep to a halt. He suffered a collapsed lung and was airlifted to a hospital. He survived the shooting and subsequently pleaded guilty to the felony of "eluding." Wash. Rev. Code Section 46.61.024(1994). By so pleading, he admitted that he drove his Jeep in a manner indicating "a wanton or willful disregard for the lives ... of others." Ibid. He subsequently brought this Section 1983 action against Brosseau.[19]

The Court looked to the decision in *Saucier* to apply in this case and said:

> Qualified immunity shields an officer from suit when she makes a decision that, even if constitutionally deficient, reasonably misapprehends the law governing the circumstances she confronted. *Saucier v. Katz*, 533 U.S., at 206 (*qualified immunity operates "to protect officers from the sometimes." hazy border between excessive and acceptable force"*). Because the focus is on whether the officer had fair notice that her conduct was unlawful, reasonableness is judged against the backdrop of the law at the time of the conduct. If the law at the time did not clearly establish that the officer's conduct would violate the Constitution, the officer should not be subject to liability or, indeed, even the burdens of litigation.[20]

Applying the rule from *Saucier* then to the facts of the case in Brosseau, the Court ruled that Brosseau's actions fell within the "hazy border between excessive and acceptable force," and that it could not be clearly established that Brosseau had violated Haugen's constitutional rights, and as such Brosseau was entitled to qualified immunity.[21]

In a discussion regarding liability of law enforcement officers we need to address the evidentiary burdens of proof. Up to this point we have discussed civil liability of law enforcement officers and governmental entities. In civil cases, the evidentiary burden of proof is significantly less than in criminal cases. The burden of proof in civil cases is by a preponderance of the evidence, more likely than not, essentially 51% certainty, that the defendant is liable. That is a relatively low burden of proof.

KEY DEFINITION 33—PREPONDERANCE OF THE EVIDENCE

In a civil case the plaintiff must prove by the preponderance of the evidence (more likely than not) that the defendant is liable for the damages caused.

In addition to a relatively low burden of proof, typically the jury does not have to be unanimous in civil cases. Usually five out of six or ten out of twelve jurors have to agree on the verdict. The burden of proof is significantly higher in a criminal case, in which the prosecution must prove the defendant's guilt beyond a reasonable doubt.

KEY DEFINITION 34—BEYOND A REASONABLE DOUBT

In a criminal case the prosecution must prove the defendant's guilt beyond a reasonable doubt. This burden is not to a certainty, but is higher than preponderance.

Jurors in criminal cases must reach a unanimous verdict. If they do not, the jury is considered to hang and the case can be tried all over again. The famous prohibition against double jeopardy does not attach until a valid verdict has been reached. Civil and criminal trials are different matters and generally double jeopardy principles do not prevent either civil or criminal cases from proceeding if a verdict has been reached in one area but not the other. Criminal trials take precedence and typically precede civil trials. Next let us examine issues regarding criminal liability of law enforcement officers.

First, a tip on reducing complaints and lawsuits—"Be nice!" It might really be simple advice, but it is certainly important. A police officer is in a sense an ambassador who must effectively relate with the public, and good communications skills are critical to achieve that end. It might be tempting for officers to focus entirely on crime fighting, but the way officers interact with the public is critical. It is so critical that after about a decade of rising complaints against New York City police officers, the NYPD made a concentrated training effort to make its officers more polite. "It includes role playing—at one recent session, cadets had to deal with actors playing out an interracial dispute, and a transgender robbery victim who was becoming hysterical—and one new but simple tactic: officers are going to start introducing themselves to people on the street."[22] While we admit that the vast majority of law enforcement officers are dedicated professionals who serve the public admirably, we also have to recognize the fact that some officers are not so conscientious.

Criminal Liability

It seems just a matter of time before an officer or police department in some jurisdiction is accused of criminal behavior. If one follows the phenomenon of police officers accused of criminal behavior over a period of years, one will find incidents all around the United States. In Seattle it appeared as if a movie, *Training Day* with Denzel Washington, had become a version of reality. A member of the Seattle Police Department, Steven Slaughter, was charged with one count of distribution of heroin, a felony punishable by 20 years in prison.[23] The Dallas Police Department fired a decorated officer after he was charged with framing innocent people with drug crimes. "Delapaz had been on paid administrative leave since January 2002, when the FBI began investigating how paid confidential informants were able to set up dozens of innocent people; mostly Mexican immigrants. They were arrested on charges that involved drugs that later turned out to be ground gypsum or some other legal substance."[24] Another formerly decorated Texas officer who framed dozens of innocent people, many of whom ended up spending many years in jail, was charged with three felony perjury charges.[25] In Miami, "The former officers were charged with conspiring to plant guns on unarmed suspects, misleading investigators about their actions and lying under oath in a vast cover-up."[26] In New York, two former detectives were convicted of murders linked to organized crime.[27] Officers in Atlanta pled guilty to charges stemming from raiding the wrong house, fatally shooting an elderly woman, and planting evidence in an attempt to cover up the botched and criminal police work.[28] In Spokane and in a case reminiscent of *Tennessee v Garner,* a police officer was charged with felony assault, among other things, after he was accused of being in a bar, off duty, and chasing an individual who the officer thought may have tried to steal his automobile, and shooting him in the back of the head as he fled. The suspect, somehow, was not fatally injured.[29]

Qualified immunity does not, and will not, shield law enforcement officers from criminal liability for criminal activity. The full range of criminal laws applies to police officers if they abuse the trust that they are given to protect the public.

Criminal liability for the most egregious actions of police officers is certainly a reality and as we can see from the incidents above,
officers can be and are charged with criminal misconduct at times.
The total number of criminal cases brought, however, is far lower than
the number of civil cases brought. That difference is due in part to the
higher standards of proof that must be met but that may not explain the
entirety of the discrepancy. Howard Rahtz[30] argues that criminal repercussions are a blunt instrument that is ultimately ill suited to judging
or reforming use of force precisely, because decisions to use force and
to determine at what level to use force are very complex. Criminal law
prefers bright-line rules, rules that simply do not exist in use of force
very often. Probably prosecutors, judges, and citizens on jury panels
are sympathetic to the complexities posed by and the dangers inherent
in the policing function. This sympathetic view coupled with complex
issues such as objective and subjective reasonableness probably leads
to fewer prosecutions being brought and fewer convictions when they
are brought.[31]

Rampart

The Rampart scandal involving the Los Angeles Police Department was
one of the most notorious cases of abuse of power by police officers and
importantly led to a consent decree between the federal Department of
Justice and the Los Angeles Police Department.

KEY DEFINITION 35—CONSENT DECREE

> In a consent decree the federal government agrees to withhold certain legal
> action against the police department if the police department agrees to a
> period of federal oversight and specific reforms within the department.

The Rampart scandal involved officers within the LAPD's antigang
unit, a CRASH unit. Officer Perez claimed members of the CRASH unit
were themselves dealing in drugs and committing crimes.[32] The federal
government investigated the charge and found evidence of serious legal
violations, a pattern or practice of excessive force and constitutional
violations that led to the consent decree.[33] The consent decree itself is

a lengthy document that required specific reforms be taken by the LAPD. All police departments should seriously consider the reforms required in the consent decree and, if a department is not adequately providing oversight of its police officers, it must consider adopting appropriate measures as outlined in the consent decree between the city of Los Angeles and the federal government. The consent decree provided for 12 significant reforms:

1. Database tracking of use of force
2. Internal Affairs-like auditing unit: Operations Headquarters Bureau (OHB)
3. Annual performance evaluations
4. Initiation of complaints procedure
5. Discipline reports
6. Internal Affairs Group (IAG)
7. Sting, random audits
8. Program for responding to people with mental illness
9. Training
10. Integrity audits
11. Inspector General audits
12. Community Outreach and Public Information efforts[34]

All police departments and even individual officers would do well to review the above list and ensure that their or their agencies' practices and procedures in some effective way cover the bases outlined above. Meaningful oversight can help prevent, detect, and limit abuse of power by particular police officers. For example, rather than relying on an all-volunteer citizen's review panel with little authority, some police departments such as Spokane are considering moving toward employing a professional ombudsman to review allegations of excessive use of force by police.[35] Spokane, and other police departments, would be moving in the right direction in making their departments' oversight more professional.

The Attorney General of the United States, pursuant to a section of the Violent Crime Control and Law Enforcement Act of 1994, can bring legal action against any law enforcement officers or organization engaged in a pattern or practice of misconduct that deprives persons of their constitutional rights. Specifically the code provides:

   (a) Unlawful conduct
      It shall be unlawful for any governmental authority, or any agent thereof, or any person acting on behalf of a governmental authority, to engage in a pattern or practice of conduct by law enforcement officers or by officials or employees of any governmental agency with responsibility for the administration of juvenile justice or the incarceration of juveniles that deprives persons of rights, privileges, or immunities secured or protected by the Constitution or the laws of the United States.

   (b) Civil action by Attorney General
      Whenever the Attorney General has reasonable cause to believe that a violation of paragraph (1) has occurred, the Attorney General, for or in the name of the United States, may in a civil action obtain appropriate equitable and declaratory relief to eliminate the pattern or practice.[36]

Section 14141 has been used by the Department of Justice to negotiate consent degrees with Los Angeles, Detroit, and Pittsburgh among others. In Detroit "the Justice Department found that Detroit's 4,200 officers were often poorly trained and some habitually made false arrests or detained people illegally."[37] These legal violations have costs the City of Detroit a great deal of money; prevention of abuse by police would be much more cost effective. "Since 1997, the city has paid at least $137 million on lawsuits filed against police."[38]

    A city's or jurisdiction's risk management polices should take into account police use of force and liability issues. The stakes are high in terms of potential monetary damages and in terms of public relations. Both private citizens and the federal government have legal tools through 1983 actions or 14141 actions to seek redress for excessive use of force by police. Acting professionally, nicely when possible, and in an objectively reasonable manner will go a long way in preventing lawsuits from occurring in the first place.

Questions for Discussion

Consider the following questions. How would you answer them?

1. How much immunity should law enforcement officers have from civil liability? What should the limits be on that immunity?
2. How much immunity should law enforcement officers have from criminal liability? What should the limits on that liability be?
3. Is a failure such as the Rampart scandal the fault of the officers involved? Is it the fault of the supervisors? Is it the fault of the law makers? Or, should officers have been singled out?

Chapter Five

High-Speed Pursuit

Introduction—*Scott v. Harris*

In March 2001, a Georgia county deputy determined the speed of a passing vehicle to be 73-miles-per-hour on a road with a 55-mile-per-hour speed limit. Responding to the speed limit violation, he pulled over behind the vehicle and activated his blue flashing lights as an indication that the driver of the vehicle should pull over. It was, up to that point, a scene that is acted out thousands of times a day across the United States: a speeder, a law enforcement officer, and a traffic stop. This time, however, things did not go according to the usual formula. Little did that deputy know that, at that point when all the issues in that pursuit were yet to be resolved, the driver of the vehicle he was pursuing was a quadriplegic and that a deputy who was to come to his assistance that night, Deputy Timothy Scott and his actions would be the subject of a case before the Supreme Court of the United States.

Instead of pulling over as expected, the vehicle driven by Victor Harris sped away, thus initiating a chase down a two-lane road at speeds exceeding 85 miles per hour.

The deputy radioed his dispatch to report that he was pursuing a fleeing vehicle, and broadcast its license plate number. Petitioner, Deputy Timothy

Scott, heard the radio communication and joined the pursuit along with other officers. In the midst of the chase, respondent pulled into the parking lot of a shopping center and was nearly boxed in by the various police vehicles. Respondent evaded the trap by making a sharp turn, colliding with Scott's police car, exiting the parking lot, and speeding off once again down a two-lane highway. Following respondent's shopping center maneuvering, which resulted in slight damage to Scott's police car, Scott took over as the lead pursuit vehicle. Six minutes and nearly 10 miles after the chase had begun, Scott decided to attempt to terminate the episode by employing a "Precision Intervention Technique ('PIT') maneuver, which causes the fleeing vehicle to spin to a stop." Having radioed his supervisor for permission, Scott was told to "'[g]o ahead and take him out.'" Instead, Scott applied his push bumper to the rear of respondent's vehicle. As a result, respondent lost control of his vehicle, which left the roadway, ran down an embankment, overturned, and crashed. Respondent was badly injured and was rendered a quadriplegic.[1]

The case that resulted from this pursuit worked its way through the federal court system after Victor Harris claimed that his Fourth Amendment rights were violated during the pursuit. Specifically, he argued that the use of the police car to force his car off the road constituted a use of deadly force that had to be viewed under the requirements established in *Garner v. Tennessee*.[2] At trial in the District Court, Deputy Scott's request for summary judgment in his favor based on an assertion of qualified immunity was denied. That decision was upheld by the Eleventh Circuit Court of Appeals in an interlocutory judgment finding that Scott's actions during the pursuit could be construed as deadly force and that the use of such force in the context of the pursuit in question would violate the right of Mr. Harris to be free from excessive force during a seizure.

The Supreme Court, in overturning the decision of the Eleventh Circuit, noted that the car chase that was initiated by Victor Harris posed "a substantial and immediate risk of serious physical injury to others" and used that fact as a basis for its finding in the case. In its decision, the Supreme Court relied on three primary factors. First, the Court reviewed the assertion of qualified immunity and decided that the facts, viewed in the light most favorable to the party alleging the injury,[3] did not show that the officer had violated a constitutional right. Second, the Court turned to the most important piece of evidence about the pursuit, a video recording by a dash-mounted camera of Deputy Scott's portion of the pursuit, as well as the portion conducted with other officers in the lead position, before Deputy Scott became involved. The Supreme Court concluded after viewing the tape that the facts represented in the tape clearly contradicted the version offered by Mr. Harris,[4] a version that they suggested, "no reasonable jury could believe."[5] Finally, the Court considered the reasonableness of Deputy Scott's actions and concluded that *Garner* had not created a bright-line rule and rigid preconditions for the imposition of deadly force. Rather, the Court argued, the law required that the force applied during a seizure be reasonable, given the circumstances and the threat posed. In applying a basic balancing test, the Court concluded that the actions of Deputy Scott were reasonable, considering the circumstances and the fact that the decision to terminate the high-speed chase in the manner that he did, did not violate the Fourth Amendment of Mr. Harris, even though it placed Mr. Harris at risk of serious injury or even death.

This case, while ultimately exonerating the actions of the officers involved, raises several serious issues surrounding high-speed pursuits that must be considered and addressed.

Definition of Pursuit and Scope of the Question

Law enforcement officers in the United States probably engage in hundreds of pursuits every day, and thousands every year.[6] Although the Hollywood type of pursuit most often covered by the media may be only a small percentage of the total,[7] significant percentage of even less dramatic pursuits results in deaths and serious injuries to suspects, law enforcement officers, and innocent bystanders and other drivers. Despite the fact that these pursuits occur with considerable frequency, there is almost no reliable data on the frequency of their occurrence or of the resulting injuries or deaths. Most states and the federal government do not currently gather data on law enforcement pursuits.

Because high-speed vehicle pursuits involve the largest weapon an officer has, namely, his vehicle, they can be considered in some cases to be an application of deadly force and for that reason, if for no other, they deserve considerable additional study. When they are engaged in a pursuit, most officers know it intuitively and many would probably feel that a specific, formal definition is unnecessary. However, to further understand the nature, scope, and problems of pursuit, such a formal definition is absolutely necessary.

KEY DEFINITION 36—PURSUIT

Pursuit may be defined as an active attempt by a law enforcement officer on duty in a patrol car to apprehend one or more occupants of a moving motor vehicle, providing the driver of such vehicle is aware of the attempt and is resisting apprehension by maintaining or increasing his speed or by ignoring the law enforcement officer's attempt to stop him.[8]

As Nugent et al. point out, this definition establishes four key points for determining whether a pursuit has occurred. First, the law enforcement officer, because he is in a patrol vehicle, is identifiable as an officer. Second, the driver of the vehicle must be aware that the officer is trying to stop him. Third, the reasons for the attempted stop may be wide-ranging, including something as minor as a traffic offense or as large as a felony. Fourth, pursuits need not be at high speed; they may in fact be at a relatively low but variable speed.[9]

By using the above definition, one can say that pursuits occur with great frequency throughout the United States and across all types of juris-dictions. It is an activity in which most officers will be engaged at some point in their career. Moreover, it is an activity that can and does result in serious injuries and death. Again, though there are few complete or reliable numbers available,[10] attempts have been made to establish how dangerous police pursuits are, not only to the officers involved but also to the individual being pursued in addition to innocent bystanders. Two studies in particular explore the dangers inherent in pursuits.

Frederick P. Rivara and Christopher Mack of the University of Washington analyzed the data reported to the Fatality Analysis Reporting System of the National Highway Traffic Safety Administration (NHTSA)[11] for the years 1994 to 2002.[12] They found that in the period reviewed, there were 2,654 fatal crashes involving 3,965 vehicles reported to that system. Those crashes killed 3,146 people, 1,088 of whom were not involved in the pursuit but innocent bystanders.[13] Rivara and Mack, in considering these data conclude that, given the dangers involved in pursuit and given that most of the individuals being pursued had prior motor-vehicle-related convictions, law enforcement should consider alternative means of detaining the offending individuals and not engage with them in pursuits.

A second study, undertaken by H. Range Hutson and his colleagues, reviews a longer timeline of the NHTSA Fatality Analysis data, 1982 through 2004.[14] This study reviewed the data in a different way and considered how the effect of variables such as alcohol consumption, road surface, and mechanism of collision affected fatalities in police pursuits. The results of this retrospective study provide an interesting view of fatalities related to police pursuits. During the period of study, 881,733 fatal crashes with a total of 987,523 fatalities were reported to the database. Of those, 6,336 fatal crashes and 7,430 total fatalities were secondary to police pursuits. The authors find that a large percentage of individuals killed had significantly elevated levels of alcohol in their blood,[15] that children and adolescents accounted for nearly one-third of all fatalities, and that blacks and Native Americans died at a higher rate per incident of pursuit.

The authors of this study conclude that pursuit-related fatalities are a small but significant percentage of total vehicle fatalities in the United States. They note, as do Rivara and Mack, that the large number of fatalities involving noninvolved individuals, as many as 27% of pursuit-related fatalities being innocent bystanders, is a matter of considerable concern and an issue that needs to be addressed at the policy and training levels. The authors provide four law-enforcement-specific recommendations related to police pursuits:

1. All states should track the annual number of cases of individuals who engage officers in pursuits, pursuit crashes, injuries, and fatalities for annual review.
2. Pursuits that occur beyond the NHTSA definition should also be identified and reviewed. State legislators should increase the penalty for individuals who engage officers in pursuits, since they pose a serious danger to public safety.

3. Police should continue to develop and utilize alternative methods such as electronic devices, helicopters, and stop strips to apprehend fleeing suspects in motor vehicles.

4. Adolescents and other high-risk groups that engage officers in pursuits should be educated about the dangers involved in this action. All law enforcement agencies in most instances should consider pursuing suspects for only suspected felony crimes.

Cases

Before the recent decision by the Supreme Court in *Scott v. Harris*, the Court had made only a few rulings that dealt specifically and explicitly with questions of pursuit. Nonetheless, these are very important decisions that have a far-reaching impact,[16] as they reverberate through not only the actuality of live pursuits but also issues of officer training and officer liability, both civil and criminal, that individual officers and the department bear as a result of pursuits.

In 1991, the Supreme Court decided the case of *California v. Hodari*[17] in which it held that police pursuit of a fleeing suspect, no matter how threatening it might seem to the suspect being pursued, does not constitute a seizure under the Fourth Amendment. According to this decision, a seizure has not occurred until the subject submits by ending the pursuit or is physically touched by an officer. Until that point, the Fourth Amendment is not implicated by the actions of the officer and therefore the officer need not be concerned with how the exclusionary rule might impact evidence discarded by the fleeing subject and recovered by law enforcement without a warrant.[18] Clearly this decision frees officers involved in pursuit to gather and retain evidence that might be discarded by a fleeing suspect without concern that the evidence might be excluded at trial. However, the more significant holding for present purposes, that a pursuit is never a seizure, needs to be considered carefully in the light of the other decisions of the Court on these issues.

As noted above, all questions of pursuit must be viewed in the light of the decision on *Tennessee v. Garner* wherein the Court had concluded that the application of deadly force is a Fourth Amendment issue per se, as it represents the most extreme form of seizure of the individual by law enforcement. It was long considered that vehicle pursuit, particularly high-speed vehicle pursuit, represented a possible application of deadly force that had to be reviewed within the *Garner* framework. While the decision in *Scott v. Harris* may appear to call that into question, the basic holding in *Garner* is still in control.

The decision in *Scott v. Harris* does not overturn or even significantly change the law related to pursuit as a seizure. While the Court in that case found ultimately in favor of the officers involved, they did so only after applying exactly the type of balancing test that is suggested in *Garner*. That is to say, the actions of the deputies in the *Harris* case were found to be justified only because specific conditions existed. The most important of them was that the subject being pursued was determined by the Court to pose a substantial and immediate risk. Only after determining that did the Court attempt to balance the danger posed by the suspect against the application of force. The application of force by Deputy Scott would not always be reasonable in pursuits; it was reasonable in this case only because the danger posed on balance warranted it.

Some applications of force within the context of a pursuit do, in fact, represent a seizure even though the pursuit has not ended and there has not been any physical contact between the officers and the suspect. The case of *Brower v. County of Inyo*[19] places some limits on the ability of law enforcement to stop fleeing suspect through the application of specific types of force. In this case, the officers in pursuit of a stolen vehicle driven by Brower chased that vehicle into a roadblock, a tractor-trailer parked across the highway in the middle of the night.

On the night of October 23, 1984, William James Caldwell (Brower) was killed when the stolen car that he had been driving at high speeds for approximately 20 miles in an effort to elude pursuing police crashed into a police roadblock. His heirs, petitioners here, brought this action in Federal District Court under 42 U.S.C. 1983, claiming, inter alia, that respondents used "brutal, excessive, unreasonable and unnecessary physical force" in establishing the roadblock, and thus effected an unreasonable seizure of Brower, in violation of the Fourth Amendment. Petitioners alleged that "under color of statutes, regulations, customs and usages," respondents (1) caused an 18-wheel tractor-trailer to be placed across both lanes of a two-lane highway in the path of Brower's flight, (2) "effectively concealed" this roadblock by placing it behind a curve and leaving it unilluminated, and (3) positioned a police car, with its headlights on, between Brower's oncoming vehicle and the truck, so that Brower would be "blinded" on his approach. App. 8-9

Petitioners further alleged that Brower's fatal collision with the truck was "a proximate result" of this official conduct.[20]

The Court was unanimous that Brower had been seized under the meaning of the Fourth Amendment by the specific and deliberate action of the officers in setting up the roadblock.

> We think it enough for a seizure that a person be stopped by the very instrumentality set in motion or put in place in order to achieve that result. It was enough here, therefore, that, according to the allegations of the complaint, Brower was meant to be stopped by the physical obstacle of the roadblock—and that he was so stopped.[21]

What distinguishes the action of the officers in this case from other actions that might not be considered to be seizures under *Hodari* is the *intentional* and complete cessation of the suspect's freedom of movement. It would have been no different for the Court if the suspect had been run off the road by the car of an officer as a means of ending the pursuit. Both are seizures.

Actions that *unintentionally* cause a restriction in the freedom of movement of a suspect do not necessarily implicate the Fourth Amendment in the same way.

> Thus, if a parked and unoccupied police car slips its brake and pins a passerby against a wall, it is likely that a tort has occurred, but not a violation of the Fourth Amendment. And the situation would not change if the passerby happened, by lucky chance, to be a serial murderer for whom there was an outstanding arrest warrant—even if, at the time he was thus pinned, he was in the process of running away from two pursuing constables. It is clear, in other words, that a Fourth Amendment seizure does not occur whenever there is a governmentally caused termination of an [489 US 593, 597] individual's freedom of movement (the innocent passerby), nor even whenever there is a governmentally caused and governmentally desired termination of an individual's freedom of movement (the fleeing felon), but only when there is a

governmental termination of freedom of movement through means intentionally applied.[22]

In other words, this roadblock was a seizure because it was intentional and because the suspect had no way to avoid being stopped by it. He was, in effect, stopped before he hit the tractor-trailer.

The Court goes further in this case, however. Applying once again the balancing test that arises from *Garner,* the court concluded not only that a seizure had occurred but also that the seizure was in fact unreasonable and that if it had resulted in Brower's death, the officers, as a result, were liable for that death.

> This is not to say that the precise character of the roadblock is irrelevant to further issues in this case. "Seizure" alone is not enough for 1983 liability; the seizure must be "unreasonable." Petitioners can claim the right to recover for Brower's death only because the unreasonableness they allege consists precisely of setting up the roadblock in such manner as to be likely to kill him.[23]

The liability found in *Brower* raises a serious issue of officer civil liability related to pursuits. As in *Scott v. Harris,* there may be some qualified immunity but that immunity extends only to a certain extent and when individual officers or whole jurisdictions are insufficiently vigilant about their policies or their training, real and significant liability can and often does result from pursuits.

A final case from the U.S. Supreme Court relates directly to the question of this liability. In *City of Canton v. Harris,*[24] the Court addressed directly the question of officer and jurisdictional liability when inadequate training produces situations that injure the constitutional rights of individuals.

> It may seem contrary to common sense to assert that a municipality will actually have a policy of not taking reasonable steps to train its employees. But it may happen that in light of the duties assigned to specific officers or employees the need for more or different training is so obvious, and the inadequacy so likely to result in the violation of constitutional rights, that the policymakers of the city can reasonably be said to have been deliberately indifferent to the need. [FN10] In that event, the failure to provide proper training may fairly be said to represent a policy for which the city is responsible, and for which the city may be held liable if it actually causes injury.[25]

Footnote 10 in the quoted passage goes on to explain the relationship between failure to train and deliberate indifference in greater detail.

> For example, city policymakers know to a moral certainty that their police officers will be required to arrest fleeing felons. The city has armed its officers with firearms, in part to allow them to accomplish this task. Thus, the need to train officers in the constitutional limitations on the use of deadly force, see *Tennessee v. Garner*, 471 US 1, 105 S. Ct. 1694, 85 L.Ed.2d 1 (1985), can be said to be "so obvious," that failure to do so could properly be characterized as "deliberate indifference" to constitutional rights.
>
> It could also be that the police, in exercising their discretion, so often violate constitutional rights that the need for further training must have been plainly obvious to the city policymakers, who, nevertheless, are "deliberately indifferent" to the need.[26]

It is certainly true that a marked police cruiser is not the firearm that the opinion talks about. It is true however that it may be no less of a deadly weapon. It is also true that, like a firearm, it can be used to assist an officer in the task of arresting a fleeing felon.

Admittedly, the standard for "deliberate indifference" as defined in *City of Canton* is very high and to prove it is a burden that any plaintiff in a civil suit would have trouble meeting.[27] However, it is also a fact that pursuits of any type are dangerous and, as has been made clear in cases such as *Brower v. County of Inyo* and *Scott v. Harris*, it can in some circumstances be considered deadly force just as the use of firearms was considered deadly force in *Garner*. Given the cases that have made that fact clear, it is implausible that any law enforcement agency could be unaware of the deadly nature of pursuits. Therefore, if municipalities or other jurisdictions fail to put in place clear policies that regulate how and when pursuits are acceptable, if those policies fail, as *Garner* requires, to balance the need for pursuits as possibly deadly force with the need to protect against unreasonable use of that force, and if agencies fail to provide adequate training for their officers, they have opened themselves and their officers up to considerable risk under Section 1983. Clearly *Garner* does matter in questions of pursuit policy, training, and performance and so law enforcement agencies need to take steps to ensure that they limit their and their officers' liability.

Policy and Training

Because of the dangers inherent in pursuits, particularly high-speed pursuits, increasing emphasis has been placed in recent years on the development of clear policies related to pursuits and increased training for officers regarding pursuit. The national trends have been toward increasing training for officers as pursuit policies are becoming more and more restrictive. These two efforts assume that fewer pursuits will mean fewer injuries and deaths and fewer lawsuits as well. The counterargument is that, moving closer to a situation in which police cannot pursue suspects at all will increase attempts to elude police because criminals will know that failing to stop will all but ensure their escape.

That argument seems largely specious. Van Blaricom writes, "The prevailing myths of the pro-chase faction are essentially two: first, if a driver runs from the police, he must have committed a more serious crime that will be discovered after apprehension and second, if we adopt a policy of not chasing everyone who runs, everyone will run. As with many honestly held beliefs, there are simply no facts to support those strongly held assumptions. To the contrary it has been demonstrated that there is neither an increase in criminality nor an increase in vehicular flight from the police that can be attributed to the adoption of a more restrictive vehicular pursuit policy."[28]

The majority of law enforcement agencies in the United States have for their officers specific policies related to pursuit. A 1997 survey conducted by Geoffrey Alpert[29] yielded some interesting results. It found that while 91% of the agencies surveyed did have pursuit policies in place, many of those policies had been created in the 1970s and were often significantly outdated. D. P. Van Blaricom[30] identifies three categories into which pursuit policies can be divided. Discretionary policies allow the officer involved in the situation to determine whether a pursuit is warranted or whether it should be continued. A discouraging policy prohibits pursuit in most cases regardless of the circumstances. The third type of policy, restrictive policy, is an attempt to balance[31] the necessity of pursuit in some cases against the real risks to the officer and others. Van Blaricom writes, "A discretionary policy is really no policy at all and leaves decision making to the ad hoc judgment of whomever happens to be engaged in the pursuit. The restrictive model incorporates the principle of balancing need against risk, as described by the IACP sample vehicular pursuit policy previously cited herein. Finally, the discouraging policy essentially prohibits all pursuits and, although in limited use, is not generally favored, as there will always be some circumstances, wherein a calculated risk must be taken to pursue for the greater necessity of apprehending an extremely dangerous criminal." [32]

Hugh Nugent et al.[33] propose four specific elements that should be present in departmental pursuit policies. First, policies should contain pursuit directives. These directives should include considerable definitional information including the definition of pursuit for the jurisdiction, the rules for initiating pursuits, the types of offenses that warrant pursuits, description of the environmental conditions under which pursuits can be initiated (times of day, weather conditions, types of roads, etc.), fixing of maximum speeds for pursuits, and explicit description of tactics that may or may not be used along with several other criteria. Second, the policy should address pursuit training. Third, every jurisdiction should have a policy on pursuit alternatives that sets down when and where they should be employed and under what circumstances. Finally, policy review and reporting requirements should be included. As might be expected, the various policies reviewed in the study showed considerable variation in how effectively these ideas were implemented.

As with all types of use of force, however, having a clear policy is only one of the factors that need to be considered. As important as the policy is the transmission of that policy to the line officers through ongoing training. It is certainly true that a lack of training increases the likelihood of pursuit-related injuries and fatalities. Any training in the area of pursuit is good but especially important is training in the real life issues related to pursuit such as the "tunnel vision" or "contempt of cop" feeling that many officers experience, resulting in their unwillingness to discontinue pursuits regardless of policy or dangers present.[34] Perhaps training officers to decide when not to pursue is at least as beneficial as training them *how* to pursue through courses in driving and other tactics in the same way that officers are not only taught how to use firearms effectively but also how to avoid using them when the situation does not demand their use. Even when officers are engaged in a pursuit, they need clear guidelines on termination of the pursuit as for example when the balance has shifted too far to justify the risks encountered.[35]

The effort to reduce the number and risk of pursuits is aided in significant ways by advances in technology. Increasing use of spike strips that can slowly deflate tires without sudden loss of control and even the development of what are called "auto arrestors"[36] promise to decrease the number and length of pursuits in the future. Controlled contact techniques including "boxing in" and "pursuit intervention techniques (PIT)" can be useful in ending pursuits, if the officers are trained and the techniques are executed and employed properly and judiciously. Incorrectly applied, these techniques can often be considered a use of deadly force. In larger jurisdictions, the helicopter as an alternative pursuit vehicle is capable of preventing not only the necessity of on-the-ground pursuits at high speeds but also of simultaneously limiting the possibility of escape by the offender. Each of these options, however, presents its own problems. Spike strips and auto arrestors must be placed in the likely path of the fleeing vehicle and deployed in a way that affects only the target vehicle. Helicopters are expensive and their use carries with it its own dangers to officers and others. One of the most effective and new advances that can be used to deter pursuits might not be technological but legislative. A simple change to state and local laws and ordinances making flight from law enforcement in a vehicle a felony rather than a misdemeanor might do more than helicopters or spike strips to stop the necessity of pursuits.

Pursuit by law enforcement is, in some senses, the ultimate use of force. It is, possibly or even frequently, an application of lethal force by an officer using the largest single piece of equipment that he uses daily. Despite that, in this area of law enforcement training is often lacking and policies are sometimes not clear. Often those failures in training and policy are a direct result of the way that pursuits and pursuit driving are perceived. The view that pursuits represent a use of force similar in many ways to the use of firearms by officers is changing, but changing slowly. It is interesting to note that many jurisdictions until recently did not even have a requirement that officers be wearing seat-belts during pursuits, something that many line officers had opposed. As policy changes are made, as they are instituted through more rigorous and ongoing training, and as better, more efficient, and more easily deployable technological aids come to the assistance of enforcement officers, fewer pursuits will be necessary and those that are, can be made increasingly safe.

Questions for Discussion

Consider the following questions. How would you answer them?

1. What do you think is a reasonable standard for pursuit? When is a pursuit, even high-speed pursuit, justified and when is it not?
2. How liable should officers be for injuries and deaths that occur during pursuits? How protected should they be from that liability?
3. What type of pursuit policy should be adopted by law enforcement agencies?
4. What types of training seem most crucial for pursuits and pursuit policies?

Conclusion:
Reasonable Use
of Force by Police

We have spent years working on this book and through those years, from time to time, people would inquire as to what we were researching and writing about. When they found out that we were working on the issue of police use of force, almost without fail, the response would be "that's timely." Indeed it is. Police use of force is always a timely issue and that says a great deal about the importance of the issue. Some incident or other was always occurring as we were working on this book. Police use of force is practically a constant issue and is likely to remain so.

What should be clear, however, is that the phrase "use of force" means something more than most people understand. Use of force is not synonymous with "excessive force" and in fact the two have little relationship. Most uses of force by law enforcement in the United States are proportional, ethical, lawful, and, above all, necessary even if not perfect. It is also true that use of force can be much more than the direct application of physical force by an officer. Many and perhaps even most uses of force by an officer are accomplished without any physical contact at all. Simply, use of force is not just fists, Tasers, batons, and firearms. Use of force can and does encompass everything from presence and command to pursuit to less lethal physical force and ultimately to the application of lethal force. Use of force requires an officer to make split-second decisions about type and level of force, to consider in stressful situations the balance between necessary force and necessary rights, and to make the right decision at first call almost every time. It is a task that is far more complex and nuanced than most people will ever realize.

One of the most important issues in writing a book such as this is deciding what to include and what to leave to others to discuss more fully. We have, throughout, cited experts, other authors, Web sites, and other resources. We would encourage you to consider reviewing any of these additional resources to further your understanding of specific topics that we have covered or as a starting point for exploring other aspects of use of force that we have had to leave aside. We have chosen to focus on a few issues, issues that we found to be most necessary to cover in coming to an understanding of the basics of application of state force by law enforcement. In selecting those topics, however, we have also had to make decision about what *not* to include in this book, for reasons of space and time. While we do not have time to deal with them in the detail they might deserve, we do want to point to some other issues to pursue in understanding the larger issues as well. All these areas of inquiry, and many others, are intimately related to use of force and use of force guidelines in the United States today.

1. *Race and Force.* This issue has come into increased prominence as questions of racial profiling have once again come to center stage. The racial divide continues to exist in the United States, as well as within the law enforcement community, despite decades of progress and best efforts to eliminate it. Increasing diversity in law enforcement agencies and increasing awareness of questions of diversity both within law enforcement as a community and within the communities that law enforcement serves will aid enormously in these areas. Volumes have been written about the questions that surround this issue but an excellent place to start an understanding is with Randall Kennedy's edited volume, *Race, Crime, and the Law*[1] and Jerome Skolnick and Jerome Fyfe's book, *Above the Law: Police and the Excessive Use of Force.*[2]

2. *Police Ethics.* There are numerous checks involved in maintaining ethical activity on the part of individual officers. From departmental controls to lawsuits to citizen review boards, the actions that officers take are being increasingly scrutinized for their ethical content. Obviously, finding new recruits to the law enforcement community who are of the highest moral character is imperative as is, once again, training them fully on questions of ethics in their profession.

3. *Use of Force Training.* The necessity of training is a theme that runs throughout this book both in general and especially in some specific areas such as pursuit training. Training allows officers in real life, stressful, life and death situations not only to make a split-second decision but also to make the *right* decision. Because of that, the importance of training cannot be overemphasized. It is also true that training needs to not only cover the gamut of use of force but also, to be most effective, integrate different aspects of force together.[3]

4. *Community Oriented Policing (COP).* COP as a model of law enforcement has become increasingly entrenched. As more and more cities and towns move toward that model, the impact that it has on use of force has begun to be considered. For a basic review of COP, Howard Rahtz's book, *Community Policing: A Handbook for Beat Cops and Supervisors,*[4] is a good place to start. For more information about the specific relationship between COP and use of force, Robert Trojanowicz's paper, "Preventing Civil Disturbances: A Community Policing Approach,"[5] provides enormous insight into how COP can lessen tension, particularly in high crime and economically depressed areas in ways that lead ultimately to less force being necessary in those areas.

Reasonable use of force by police is what society and the law expect and reasonable use of force is what law enforcement officers typically strive to employ and, in the vast majority of cases, police employ force reasonably, legally, and ethically. It is not always easy for the public, media, lawyers, and police to determine what constitutes reasonable use of force by police, given particular fact patterns. We hope that the preceding chapters help to add to the understanding of what does constitute reasonable use of force by police, as well as what constitutes excessive use of force. Circumstances and technology are likely to change and present unique problems and questions as well as new possible answers. Just as the introduction of the TASER to modern policing has simultaneously reduced firearm use *and* created new problems in use of force, any new advance in technology is likely to provide both problems and promise for officers on the street.

If the goal of law enforcement as an institution and the desire of individual officers are the same, that is, to use force appropriately, there is no substitute for training. Without a doubt, training is the key element in preventing excesses in use of force while allowing officers to proactively do their jobs as safely and efficiently as possible. Training, however, must be based on clear policies and procedures. Whether those policies are departmental or agency level policies or they are state or federal statues, they must be clear, they must be as unambiguous as possible, and they must be taught. It is that link between clear effective policy and ongoing training that will allow officers on the ground to employ force as necessary but in a way that is ultimately fair and respectful of the necessity to protect the rights of individual citizens as well.

One test—to determine fairness and justice (and often legality)— should endure, and that is considering the totality of the circumstances: Was the use of force by law enforcement objectively reasonable? Hopefully the answer will typically be a clear and straightforward "yes." If the answer is "no," at the least there will probably be an outcry from the public and media and quite possibly civil and or criminal legal actions for the officer and department to deal with. Sometimes the answer is "maybe" and that is a hard one. A "maybe:" for an answer may as well be a "no," practically, as the consequences of a maybe are likely to be about the same as a no. It behooves law enforcement to act in an objectively reasonable manner. Doing that requires that each officer on the ground keeps key portions of the Bill of Rights for law enforcement in mind.

KEY PORTIONS OF THE BILL OF RIGHTS

Amendment IV

The right of the people to be secure in their persons, houses, papers, and effects, against unreasonable searches and seizures, shall not be violated, and no Warrants shall issue, but upon probable cause, supported by Oath or affirmation, and particularly describing the place to be searched, and the persons or things to be seized.

Amendment V

No person shall be ... compelled in any criminal case to be a witness against himself, nor deprived of life, liberty, or property, without due process of law.

Amendment VI

In all criminal prosecutions, the accused shall enjoy the right to a speedy and public trial, ... and to be informed of the nature and cause of the accusation; to be confronted with the witnesses against him; to have compulsory process for naming witnesses in his favor, and to have the Assistance of Counsel for his defense.

Amendment VIII

Excessive bail shall not be required, nor excessive fines imposed, nor cruel and unusual punishments inflicted.

For line officers to be able to perform their jobs as effectively and safely as possible those constitutional standards must be incorporated carefully and thoughtfully into policies that can be utilized by those officers to keep us all safe.

Glossary of Key Definitions

1983 Action: A 1983 action is a federal civil suit that alleges that an officer, police department, or governmental agency wrongfully violated the plaintiff's constitutional rights.

21-Foot Rule: A noncompliant individual within 21 feet of an officer can create an imminent danger to the officer. A hostile individual within 21 feet armed with a knife, blunt instrument, or even with fists can present an imminent danger as the hostile individual could close that 21-foot distance faster than an officer might be able to react.

After Action Review: An after action review is an exercise of reflection immediately after the event. It is a critical analysis of what went right, what went wrong, what was not expected, and what the actors would do next time.

Allowable Traffic Stops: Traffic stops made on the basis of probable cause are valid allowable stops, regardless of the officer's subjective intentions. These stops represent temporary seizures of the vehicle and its occupants but are not considered custodial interrogations under the current law.

Arrest: Arrest is a narrower concept than seizure; it is a specific and very serious kind of seizure. All that is required is some affirmative action by the officer to detain or to take actual control of the person. Arrest is said to have occurred when a reasonable person would feel that, having been detained, he or she was not free to leave or otherwise decline the officer's request.

Beyond a Reasonable Doubt: In a criminal case the prosecution must prove the defendant's guilt beyond a reasonable doubt. This burden is not to a certainty, but is higher than preponderance.

Consent Decree: In a consent decree the federal government agrees to withhold certain legal action against the police department if the police department agrees to a period of federal oversight and specific reforms within the department.

Consent: Consent involves an agreement or willingness on the part of the individual that an invasion of a right may occur. A person can waive any constitutional right that they have, if that waiver is made knowingly, intelligently, and voluntarily.

Custody and Arrest: "[T]he appropriate inquiry is whether a reasonable person would feel free to decline the officers' requests or otherwise terminate the encounter." If the answer is "no," then the individual is in custody.

Due Process: Due process is guaranteed by the Fifth and Fourteenth Amendments. Procedural due process requires notice, a hearing, and an opportunity to be heard. Substantive due process requires actual fairness in proceedings. Due process essentially requires fairness. Violation of due process can be argued when procedure or substance is not fair.

Duty to Render Aid after Use of Force: After use of force if it appears reasonably necessary to summon aid, then officers should render and summon appropriate aid within a reasonable time.

Engagement Drill: An engagement drill is similar to a military battle drill. Officers practice responding to simulated scenarios to hone their reactions and refine their judgment.

Exclusionary Rule: The rule requires that "All evidence obtained by searches and seizures in violation of the Constitution is, by that same authority, inadmissible in a state court."

Exigent Circumstances: Exigent circumstances are emergency circumstances in which time is of the essence and there is imminent danger to people or possibly to evidence. In seizure and arrest, this usually refers to situations in which the officer would be unable to effectuate the arrest or seize the necessary evidence unless he or she acts swiftly and without prior judicial approval.

Garrity Statement: When an officer is forced to make a statement under the threat of possibly losing his job, the officer can make a statement but that statement cannot be used against him in a criminal matter.

Graham Factors in Use of Force:

1. The severity of the Crime.
2. Whether the suspect posed an immediate threat to the safety of officers or others.
3. Whether the suspect is actively resisting.
4. Whether the suspect is attempting to evade arrest by flight.

Immunity of Law Enforcement Officers: Law enforcement officers enjoy qualified immunity from laws regarding use of force, if that use of force is reasonable, necessary, and appropriate and in the course of executing official duties. Qualified immunity is thus a shield for law enforcement officers, but the shield is not absolute; excessive force is not shielded.

Interrogation: "The term 'interrogation' under Miranda refers not only to express questioning, but also to any words or actions on the part of police (other than those normally attendant to arrest and custody) that the police should know are reasonably likely to elicit an incriminating response from the suspect."

Lethal Force (Appropriate Use of): An officer can use deadly force only when he reasonably believes that his life or another's life is in danger, or if he reasonably believes that he or another faces grave bodily injury and that no reasonable alternative to the use of that force appeared to exist at the time.

Miranda Warning: Prior to any questioning, the person must be warned that he has a right to remain silent, that any statement that he does make may be used as evidence against him, and that he has a right to the presence of an attorney, either retained, or appointed.

Objectively Reasonable: Objectively reasonable requires assessment by a third party to ask whether a hypothetically reasonable person in the actor's situation would have acted as he did. This is a higher standard than subjectively reasonable, as one must consider what a reasonable person would have done; it does not assume that the actor was in fact a reasonable person. Objectively reasonable is the more common legal standard.

Operation Order: The operation order is a standard format for organizing and planning police action and use of force. Operations orders may be issued for a variety of situations but are crucial whenever any law enforcement officer or agency responds to crowd control or siege incident.

Plain View: Whenever an officer observes something illegal that is held out to the public, or, if the officer is somewhere he has a right to be and observes something illegal in plain view, he may determine probable cause and arrest the individual and seize the evidence without a warrant. There is no reasonable expectation of privacy to something in plain view.

Preponderance of the Evidence: In a civil case the plaintiff must prove by the preponderance of the evidence (more likely than not) that the defendant is liable for the damages caused.

Probable Cause: Probable cause is a set of trustworthy facts or information that objectively gives the officer or judge a reasonable belief that a crime *likely* is being committed or *likely* has been committed. Those facts need not be sufficient to establish guilt but they must be more than mere suspicion. Probable cause necessary for arrest and seizures and searches is greater than the reasonable suspicion that a crime might be committed necessary for Terry Stops.

Proportionality: Proportional means appropriate and fair. Proportional action is action that fits the circumstance, action that was appropriate to the circumstance. A proportional response is in proper relationship to the event.

Pursuit: Pursuit may be defined as an active attempt by a law enforcement officer on duty in a patrol car to apprehend one or more occupants of a moving motor vehicle, provided the driver of such vehicle is aware of the attempt and is resisting apprehension by maintaining or increasing his speed or by ignoring the law enforcement officer's attempt to stop him.

Ready Mobility of Vehicle: Ready mobility of a vehicle creates an exigent circumstance that allows officers to search a vehicle without a warrant, if officers have probable cause for the traffic stop and if officers have probable cause to believe the object of their search will be found in the automobile.

Reasonable Suspicion: Reasonable Suspicion is sufficient to provide Fourth Amendment justification for an officer temporarily seizing an individual provided that there is, "a particularized and objective basis, supported by specific and articuable facts, for *suspecting* a person of criminal activity."

Reasonable: "Fair, proper, just, moderate, or suitable under the circumstances" "not immoderate or excessive" "under the influence of reason, amenable to reason."

Right to Counsel: If a suspect in custody indicates that he wishes to talk to an attorney before speaking, there can be no questioning.

Seizure: Seizure is a broad concept including detentions, brief or lengthy, of property or people. The term implies the removal of something from the possession of another or removing the freedom of movement in the case of an individual being seized. A law enforcement officer may briefly seize or detain an individual and may do so with less than probable cause for purposes of a brief investigation. Higher standards are required to make full arrests.

Statute of Limitations: A statute of limitations is a time period that, once expired, prevents further legal action from being brought. There is a civil and criminal statute of limitations for all legal actions except murder. The statute of limitations in a civil tort case is typically between two and four years. One must be aware of the statute of limitations. Its expiration is an absolute bar to legal action and it is a common and successful defense to legal actions.

Subjectively Reasonable: An assessment of reasonableness based on what the actor believes to be or have been reasonable. If he believes that he acted reasonably then the action is subjectively reasonable.

Terry Stop:

"Where a police officer
1. Observes unusual conduct which leads him reasonably to conclude in light of his experience that criminal activity may be afoot and
2. That the persons with whom he is dealing may be armed and dangerous,

Where in the course of investigating this behavior he
1. Identifies himself as a policeman and
2. Makes reasonable inquiries, and

If nothing in the initial stages of the encounter serves to dispel his reasonable fear for his own or others' safety, he is entitled for the protection of himself and others in the area to conduct a carefully limited search of the outer clothing of such persons in an attempt to discover weapons which might be used to assault him. Such a search is a reasonable search under the Fourth Amendment, and any weapons seized may properly be introduced in evidence against the person from whom they were taken."

Use of Force (By Police): Use of Force by police is any expression of force that is meant to produce specific law-enforcement-related results. These expressions can include physical, uniformed police presence (at the minimal end of the continuum on use of force), flashing patrol car lights, foot or vehicle pursuit, use of fists and holds, batons, aerosols, Tasers, less lethal projectiles, water cannons, and firearms (at the maximum end of the continuum on use of force).

Key Cases and Holdings

Brower v. County of Inyo, 489 U.S. 593 (1989). This case places some limits on the ability of law enforcement to stop fleeing suspect through the application of specific types of force. "We think it enough for a seizure that a person be stopped by the very instrumentality set in motion or put in place in order to achieve that result. It was enough here, therefore, that, according to the allegations of the complaint, Brower was meant to be stopped by the physical obstacle of the roadblock and that he was so stopped." What distinguishes the action of the officers in this case from other actions that might not be considered to be seizures under *Hodari* is the *intentional* and complete cessation of the suspect's freedom of movement. It is for the Court, no different if the suspect has been run off the road by the car of an officer as a means of ending the pursuit. Both are seizures.

California v. Hodari, 111 S.Ct. 1547 (1991). The Supreme Court held that police simply pursuing of a fleeing suspect, no matter how threatening that pursuit might seem to the suspect being pursued, does not constitute a seizure under the Fourth Amendment. According to the Court in the decision, a seizure has not occurred until the subject submits by ending the pursuit or is physically touched by an officer. Until that point, the Fourth Amendment is not implicated by the actions of the officer and therefore the officer need not be concerned with how the exclusionary rule might impact evidence discarded by the fleeing subject and recovered by law enforcement without a warrant.

Canton v. Harris, 489 U.S. 378 (1989). This case allows a plaintiff to file a civil lawsuit alleging that a police department's lack of training constituted a policy that led to a deprivation of the plaintiff's constitutional rights. In the case, the Supreme Court used the term "deliberate indifference" as the standard of misconduct that the plaintiff would have to prove in a 1983 action. "We hold today that the inadequacy of police training may serve as the basis for 1983 liability only where failure to train amounts to deliberate indifference to the rights of persons with whom the police come into contact used the term." Specifically with regard to pursuits, the Court held, "For example, city policymakers know to a moral certainty that their police officers will be required to arrest fleeing felons. The city has armed its officers with firearms, in part to allow them to accomplish this task. Thus, the need to train officers in the constitutional limitations on the use of deadly force, see *Tennessee v. Garner*, 471 U.S. 1, 105 S.Ct. 1694, 85 L.Ed.2d 1 (1985), can be said to be 'so obvious,' that failure to do so could properly be characterized as 'deliberate indifference' to constitutional rights."

Florida v. Bostick, 501 U.S. 429 (1991). This case sets a legal standard and definition for the term "arrest," a completely custodial state. "[T]he appropriate inquiry is whether a reasonable person would feel free to decline the officers' requests or otherwise terminate the encounter." If a reasonable person would not feel free to walk away, ignoring the officer, then the individual is in custody.

Garrity v. New Jersey, 385 U.S. 493 (1967). Law enforcement officers also have a right to be free from coercive interrogations and to have the fruits of coercive interrogations excluded from future criminal actions against them. When an officer is forced to make a statement under the threat of possibly losing his job, the officer can make a statement but that statement cannot be used against him in a criminal matter.

Graham v. Conner, 490 U.S. 386 (1989). The Supreme Court recognized that the use of force by police is situational. The decision gives considerable deference to the circumstances faced by police but clearly holds police accountable for their use of force, deadly or otherwise, through employment of an objectively reasonable standard. "[T]the 'reasonableness' inquiry in an excessive force case is an objective one; the question is whether the officers' actions are 'objectively reasonable' in light of the facts and circumstances confronting them, without regard to their underlying intent or motivation."

Katz v. United States, 389 U.S. 347 (1967). This case affirms the right of privacy held by individuals under the Constitution but also limits the scope of that right by creating what is known as the "plain view rule." The Court made it clear in Katz that "the Fourth Amendment protects people, not places. What a person knowingly exposes to the public, even in his own home or office, is not a subject of Fourth Amendment protection. But what he seeks to preserve as private, even in an area accessible to the public, may be constitutionally protected."

Kyllo v. United States, 533 U.S. 27 (2001). Justice Scalia summed up the question presented. He wrote that "[t]his case presents the question of whether the use of a thermal-imaging device aimed as a private home from a public street to detect relative amounts of heat within the home constitutes a 'search' within the meaning of the Fourth Amendment." In its opinion, the Supreme Court argued, "[w]e think that obtaining by sense-enhancing technology any information regarding the interior of the home that could not otherwise have been obtained without physical 'intrusion into a constitutionally protected area' … constitutes a search—at least where(as here) the technology in question is not in general public use." In short, technology cannot necessarily be used to avoid constitutional limitations that would exist in the absence of that technology.

Mapp v. Ohio, 367 U.S. 643. This case extended the basic holding from *Weeks v. United States* by incorporating the exclusionary rule found in that case against state power as well. *Weeks* had prohibited only the national government from using illegally seized evidence and *Mapp* extended that to also limit the power of state governments in the same way.

Miranda v. Arizona (consolidated with *Westover v. United States, Vignera v. New York, and California v. Stewart*), 384 U.S. 436 (1966). Although controversial when first decided, the rule enunciated in *Miranda* has become a well-known and important rule of criminal procedure law regarding custodial interrogation. Stated simply, the Miranda rule sets the parameters for custodial interrogation. "Prior to any questioning, the person must be warned that he has a right to remain silent, that any statement that he does make may be used as evidence against him, and that he has a right to the presence of an attorney, either retained or appointed. The defendant may waive effectuation of these rights, provided the waiver is made voluntarily, knowingly and intelligently. If, however, he indicates in any manner and at any stage of the process that he wishes to consult with an attorney before speaking there can be no questioning. Likewise, if the individual is alone and indicates in any manner that he does not wish to be interrogated, the police may not question him. The mere fact that he may have answered some questions or volunteered some statements on his own does not deprive him of the right to refrain from answering any further inquiries until he has consulted with an attorney and thereafter consents to be questioned."

Rhode Island v. Innis, 446 U.S. 291 (1980). When officers control the time, place, and manner of the atmosphere and manipulate the atmosphere to gain an incriminating response from the suspect Miranda concerns may come into play, despite the fact that the officers may have never addressed the subject. "[T]he Miranda safeguards come into play whenever a person in custody is subjected to either express questioning or its functional equivalent. That is to say, the term 'interrogation' under Miranda refers not only to express questioning, but also to any words or actions on the part of police (other than those normally attendant to arrest and custody) that the police should know are reasonably likely to elicit an incriminating response from the suspect."

Saucier v. Katz, 533 U.S. 194 (2001). This case holds that qualified immunity for law enforcement officers can operates "to protect officers from the sometimes 'hazy border between excessive and acceptable force.'" The Court ruled that "an officer may be protected by qualified immunity even if a violation of individual rights or an improper application of force was present provided that there was a reasonable though incorrect belief on the part of the officer involved." [E]ven if a court were to hold that the officer violated the Fourth Amendment by conducting an unreasonable, warrantless search, *Anderson* still operates to grant officers immunity for reasonable mistakes as to the legality of their actions. The same analysis is applicable in excessive force cases, where in addition to the deference officers receive on the underlying constitutional claim, qualified immunity can apply in the event the mistaken belief was reasonable.

Scott v. Harris (no. 05–1631) Argued February 26, 2007—Decided April 30, 2007. The Court considered the reasonableness of Deputy Scott's decision to ram from behind the vehicle driven by Mr. Harris under the requirements found in *Garner v. Tennessee*. The Court concluded that *Garner* had not created a bright-line rule and rigid preconditions for the imposition of deadly force. Rather, the Court argued, the law required that the force applied during a seizure be reasonable, given the circumstances and the threat posed. In applying a basic balancing test, the Court concluded that the actions taken were reasonable because of the circumstances, including, "a substantial and immediate risk of serious physical injury to others" and that the decision to terminate the high-speed chase in the manner that he did, did not violate the Fourth Amendment of Mr. Harris even though it placed him at risk of serious injury or even death.

Tennessee v. Garner, 471 U.S. 1 (1985). The *Garner* case limits the authority of law enforcement to utilize force in some instances. "The use of deadly force to prevent the escape of all felony suspects, whatever the circumstances, is constitutionally unreasonable. It is not better that all felony suspects die than they escape. Where the suspect poses no immediate threat to the officer and no threat to others, the harm resulting from failing to apprehend him does not justify the use of deadly force to do so. It is no doubt unfortunate when a suspect who is in sight escapes, but the fact that the police arrive a little late or are a little slower afoot does not always justify killing the suspect. A police officer may not seize an unarmed, non-dangerous suspect by shooting him dead."

Terry v. Ohio, 392 U.S. 1 (1968). In this case, the Supreme Court extended the power of law enforcement to include what have become know as "Terry Stops." In instances where an officer has a reasonable suspicion that criminal activity may be ongoing and where he has reasonable fear for his safety or the safety of others, he may briefly detain or seize the individuals he reasonably believes to be involved in that activity and ask questions of them. If the answers are not sufficient to allay the officer's reasonable fear that the individuals may be armed, the officer may, for purposes of protection of himself and others, conduct a careful and limited search of the individuals. A Terry Stop may well lead to the officer's formation of probable cause to make an arrest, depending on the circumstances. Evidence reasonably discovered during that search is generally admissible and not subject to exclusion at trial.

Weeks v. United States, 232 U.S. 383 (1914). This case established the exclusionary rule which, on the basis of the Fourth Amendment provides that evidence seized as a result of an illegal search or seizure cannot be used against a defendant. For example, if police enter a home without probable cause, consent, or a warrant, and seizure of evidence occurs, then that evidence must be excluded from trial or other legal proceedings. Further, evidence found because of or as a result of the initial illegally obtained evidence is also inadmissible as it is considered tainted as "fruit of the poisonous tree."

Whren v. United States, 517 U.S. 806 (1996). This case deals with the probable cause standard for traffic stops and rejects the idea that the subjective intentions of the officer are more important for determining if a constitutional violation has occurred. The Court determined that whatever the subjective intentions of the officers, if the objective standard of probable is satisfied then the evidence seized is admissible. "Subjective intentions play no role in the ordinary, probable cause Fourth Amendment analysis ... there is no realistic alternative to the common law rule that probable cause justifies a search and seizure ... the officers had probable cause to believe that petitioners had violated the traffic code. That rendered the stop reasonable under the Fourth Amendment, the evidence they discovered admissible."

Notes

Introduction:
Understanding Use of Force

1. While this book focuses largely on the use of force by the individual officer, the role of administrative policymaking should not be entirely discounted. Studies suggest that limitation at a policy level can have a profound impact on officer decisions in particular situations. For a more complete discussion of the importance of the use of administrative policy as a limitation on use of force decisions, see Michael White, "Controlling Police Decisions to Use Deadly Force: Reexamining the Importance of Administrative Policy," *Crime and Delinquency* 47(1): 131–151.

2. Hector Castro, *Cops Call Taser a Lifesaver*, Seattle PI.nwsource.com, November 30, 2004.

3. "Slain Teen Had BB Gun," *Spokesman-Review*, by Kevin Graman, September 29, 2003.

4. See Jess Walter. 2002. *Ruby Ridge*. New York: HarperCollins.

5. For the most complete and detailed account of the Ruby Ridge incident, see Jess Walter. 2002. *Ruby Ridge*. New York: HarperCollins.

6. Jerome Slotnick and James Fyfe. 1993. *Above the Law: Police and the Excessive Use of Force*. New York: Free Press. 37.

7. The Bureau of Justice statistics reports on the number of citizen complaints about use of force by law enforcement. In its 2006 report, the Bureau reports on 26,556 citizen complaints filed in 2002 against large state and local law enforcement agencies (those with more than 100 sworn officers). Of those complaints, 34% were not

sustained on further review, 25% were found to be unfounded, 23% resulted in the officer being exonerated, and only 8% were substantiated. While not a complete picture and while it must be viewed with some caution, this report does suggest that, in general in the agencies reviewed, citizen claims about the use of excessive force are seldom substantiated, even by civilian complaint review boards. (U.S. Department of Justice, Office of Justice Programs, Bureau of Justice Statistics. 2006. *Citizen Complaints about Police Use of Force*. Available online at http://www.ojp.usdoj. gov/bjs/abstract/ccpuf.htm).

8. An excellent review of excessive or unreasonable force information can be found in William Geller and Hans Toch. 1996. *Police Violence*. New Haven: Yale University Press.

9. In his 1987 work, James Fyfe argues that there are three primary variables that impact law enforcement use of force decisions and by extension, excessive uses of force by police: Environmental factors, Organizational factors, and Situational variables. See James Fyfe. 1988. "Police Shooting: Environment and License" in *Controversial Issues in Crime and Justice*, J. E. Scott and T. Hirschi, eds., Newbury Park, CA: Sage Publications.

10. For a complete discussion of the difficulty in compiling and discussing data about use of force by law enforcement, see Tom McEwen. 1996. *National Data Collection on Police Use of Force*. It is available online at http://www.ojp.usdoj.gov/bjs/pub/pdf/ndcopuof.pdf.

1. Seizure, Searches, Probable Cause, and Arrest

1. Some discount mere uniformed presence as a true use of force and this points again to the definitional problems inherent in discussions of use of force as such. We choose to include it here because many law enforcement agencies include it in their training. It is often taught as "Command Presence," as a means of gaining compliance without the necessity of additional physical force. Certainly the badge, gun, uniform, and official vehicle are attempts to project official force in a nonphysical manner.

2. Fourth Amendment, United States Constitution, 1791.

3. *Weeks v. United States*, 232 US 383 (1914).

4. See *Wong Sun v. United States*, 371 US 471 (1963).

5. The protection of individual rights through the exclusionary rule and its extension in cases such as *Mapp* have traditionally been thought to be beneficial to law enforcement, providing them an affirmative means of demonstrating that the procedural protection of the individual rights has been accomplished. To bolster this general argument, several studies have shown that very few cases

are lost as a result of evidence being excluded on *Mapp* or *Miranda* grounds (see, for example, the National Institutes of Justice study, 1983. *The Effects of the Exclusionary Rule: A Study in California,* U. S. Department of Justice). More recent studies have begun to question those assumptions and the methods used to support them. Focusing less on cases lost or cases diverted, more recent studies have looked at the effect that these exclusionary practices have on criminal behavior and some have concluded on the basis of an economic modeling process that crime rates have actually increased as a result of extending the exclusionary rule (see, for example, Raymond Atkins and Paul Rubin. 1999. *Effects of Criminal Procedure: Mapping Out the Consequences of the Exclusionary Rule*).

6. *Mapp v. Ohio,* 367 US 643, at 655 (1961).
7. Jude Harold Rothwax. 1997. *Guilty: The Collapse of Criminal Justice,* Warner Books. 43; see also *Mapp v. Ohio,* 367 US 643 (1961).
8. See *Hudson v. Michigan,* no. 04–1360. Argued January 9, 2006, reargued May 18, 2006, and decided June 15, 2006.
9. *Terry v. Ohio,* 392 US 1 (1968).
10. *Blacks Law Dictionary,* 1999. 7th edition, St. Paul, MN: West Group. 1273. (Emphasis added); Reasonable suspicion necessary for Terry Stop.
11. *Terry v. Ohio,* 392 US 1 (1968).
12. *Terry v. Ohio,* 392 US 1, at 30–31 (1968).
13. Terry Stop principles apply to traffic stops also. See *Michigan v. Long,* 463 US 1032 (1983).
14. *United States v. Watson,* 423 US 411 (1976).
15. *United States v. Watson,* 423 US 411 (1976).
16. See "Justices Back Police Intervention without a Warrant," Linda Greenhouse, *New York Times,* A22, May 23, 2006; see also *Brigham City v. Stuart* (no. 05–502) argued April 24, 2006, decided May 22, 2006.
17. See *Florida v. Bostick,* 501 US 429 (1991).
18. "Texas Court Rebuked on Illegal Arrest," Linda Greenhouse, *New York Times,* May 5, 2003.
19. "Texas Court Rebuked on Illegal Arrest," Linda Greenhouse, *New York Times,* May 5, 2003.
20. See *Schneckloth v. Bustamonte,* 412 US 218 (1973) regarding consent to search a car; see *Brewer v. Williams et al.,* 474 US 159 (1985) regarding right to waive right to counsel see *Miranda v. Arizona et al.,* 384 U. S. 436 (1966) and; regarding right to waive right to remain silent, see *McMann v. Richardson, et al.,* 397 US 759 (1970), effect if guilty plea forfeiting (not necessarily waiving) right to trial.
21. See, for example, *Boyd v. United States* (1888), Justice Brandeis' dissent in *Olmstead v. United States* (1928), and particularly *Griswold v. Connecticut* (1965) in which case the Supreme Court formally declared a right of privacy to be found in the Constitution.

22. *Katz v. United States*, 389 US 347 (1967).

23. See *Harris v. United States*, 390 US 234 (1947) and *Washington v. Chrisman*, 455 US 1 (1982).

24. *California v. Greenwood*, 486 US 35 (1988).

25. *California v. Greenwood*, 486 US 35, at 37–38 (1988).

26. *Kyllo v. United States*, 533 US 27, at 29–30 (2001).

27. *Kyllo v. United States*, 533 US 27, at 29 (2001).

28. *Kyllo v. United States*, 533 US 27, at 34, citing *Silverman*, 365 US at 512 (2001).

29. A complete discussion of the relationship between police and ethics can be found in Edwin Delattre. 1996. *Character and Cops*. Washington DC: AEI Press.

30. Video tapes such as "Professional Ethics in Law Enforcement" S4V1 by ALERT Publishing, Inc. help to raise questions about morality and ethics in policing and provide good discussion material.

2. Use of Lethal and Nonlethal Force

1. Recent national data on the use of force by law enforcement are not readily available. Section 210402 of the Violent Crime Control and Law Enforcement Act of 1994 requires the Attorney General to "acquire data about the use of excessive force by law enforcement officers" and to "publish an annual summary of the data acquired." The national legislature has refused to fund that collection for the past several years and, as a result, many of the data available are fast becoming dated. The National Institute of Justice suggests that the problems will not be lessened in the near future. "Systematically collecting information on use of force from the Nation's more than 17,000 law enforcement agencies is difficult given the lack of standard definitions, the variety of incident recording practices, and the sensitivity of the issue." Department of Justice, National Institute of Justice. 1996. *National Data Collection on Police Use of Force*, National Institute of Justice. vi. Available online at http://www.ojp.gov/bjs/pub/pdf/ndcopuof.pdf.

2. International Association of Chiefs of Police, *SPD Special Report: Use of Force by Seattle Police Department Officers*, 2001). Online at: http://www.theiacp.org/research/CuttingEdge/SeattlePDUseofForce.pdf.

3. Bureau of Justice Statistics, U.S. Department of Justice. 2005. *Contacts between Police and the Public*. Available online at http://www.ojp.usdoj.gov/bjs/abstract/cpp05.htm.

4. See Joel Garner et al. "Measuring the Continuum of Force Used by and Against the Police," *Criminal Justice Review* 20(2): 146–168.

5. Use of physical force may involve a wide range of activities and actions by officers. In addition to the more obvious uses of force discussed here, physical force may include things such as utilizing police dogs, a highly specialized use of force that

for most situations serves to unnecessarily complicate use of force continuum for most officers. Most officers are more likely to require uses of force that are more consistent with the continuum provided here.

6. Consider also the larger use of force continuum held out as a model by the federal law enforcement training center consisting of five levels of threat and use of force:

	Reasonable Officer Response	Reasonable Officer Perception of Threat
Level five	Deadly force	Serious bodily harm/death
Level four	Defensive tactics	Assaultive
Level three	Compliance techniques	Resistant
Level two	Contact controls	Passive
Level one	Communication skills	Complacent

"Use of Force" in DVD format, Discovery Education, AIMS Multimedia, hosted by Ed Nowicki, illustrates and explains very well the federal use of force model continuum and in addition provides a good overview of police use of force generally.

7. A series of reports in the *Washington Post* (Craig Whitlock and David Fallis, *Washington Post*, July 1 to July 4, 2001) in 2001 provided data on 11 years of police shootings for 50 large law enforcement agencies. The data show a very low rate of police use of firearms in fatal shootings; a median rate of only 0.60 fatal shootings per 10,000 arrests made for the 50 agencies, only 3.36 fatal shootings per 10,000 violent crimes for the 50 agencies reviewed and only 0.94 fatal shootings per 1000 violent crime arrests. Placed in the context of almost 44 million Americans having contact with the police annually the rate of the use of force is less than 1%. Thus, while clearly important as a use of force by police, use of explicitly lethal force must be viewed as only one expression of force even in violent crime arrests, and a relatively rare one at that. These data comport closely with earlier studies of police use of force (see, for example, U.S. Department of Justice, Office of Justice Programs. 1999. "Use of Force by Police: Overview of National and Local Data." Available online at http://www.ojp.usdoj.gov/bjs/abstract/ufbponld.htm).

8. IE see the NYPD Patrol Guide, 2004 edition, PG 203-12 Deadly Physical Force; see also FLETC MANUAL 91–01.A USE OF FORCE POLICY AND GUIDELINES 2. (e).

9. *Tennessee v. Garner*, 471 US 1, at 3-4 (1985).

10. *Tennessee v. Garner*, 471 US 1, at 11 (1985). Emphasis added.

11. See, for example, *Tennessee v. Garner*, 471 US 1 (1985).

12. In the State of Washington, for instance, the Revised Code of Washington defines "Necessary" as meaning that no reasonably effective alternative to the use of force

appeared to exist and that the amount of force used was reasonable to effect the lawful purpose intended (RCW 9A.16.010[1]).

13. The video tape "Shoot/ Don't Shoot" hosted by Peter Faulk, Coronet/MTI Films and Video, though somewhat dated, illustrates the timeless dilemmas of the quick and difficult decisions that officers must make when deciding whether to use deadly force.

14. *Blacks Law Dictionary.* 1999. 7th edition. St. Paul, MN: West Group. 1272.

15. Washington Revised Code 9A.16.010 (1) 2001.

16. See *Graham v. Conner*, 490 US 386 (1989), where the Supreme Court held, "All claims that law enforcement officials have used excessive force—deadly or not—in the course of an arrest, investigatory stop, or other 'seizure' of a free citizen are properly analyzed under the Fourth Amendment's 'objective reasonableness' standard, rather than under a substantive due process standard."

17. See the case of *Graham v. Conner*, 490 US 386 (1989).

18. *See People v. Goetz,* 497 N.E.2d 41 (1986).

19. George P. Fletcher. 1990. *A Crime of Self Defense.* Chicago: University of Chicago Press.

20. Mens Rea is a component of criminal responsibility. It can be defined as "a guilty mind" or "a guilty or wrongful purpose." It is required for intent to exist.

21. *Graham v Conner*, 490 US 386, at 389–390 (1989).

22. *Graham v Connor*, 490 US 386, at 395–396 (1989).

23. These data are taken from Charlie Mesloh, Mark Henych, Steve Hogland, and Frank Thompson. 2005. "TASER and Less Lethal Weapons: An Exploratory Analysis of Deployment and Effectiveness," *Law Enforcement Executive Forum* 5(5): 67–79.

24. The most useful resource concerning less lethal options for law enforcement is www.less-lethal.org, a Web site created cooperatively by the International Association of Chiefs of Police, the Office of Community Oriented Policing at the Department of Justice, and the National Institute of Justice. It serves as a clearing house for information on less lethal force options including policy papers and academic research papers.

25. For discussion-related issues, see Robinson, Paul H. 2005 "Does the Availability of Effective Non-Lethal Weapons Make the Use of Firearms in Defense Unlawful? Does It Mean the Rise of NLW Cowboys?" Available at the Social Science Research Network at http://ssrn.com/abstract=844389.

26. A Federal Appellate Court has made it clear that there is no necessary duty to use or even consider the use of less lethal options in every situation. See, for example, *Plakas v. Drinski*, 19 F.3d 1143 (7th Cir. 1994). The court was clear in that case that if the conduct of a suspect warrants the use of deadly force, the officer need not resort to a less deadly alternative before employing deadly force. "[W]here deadly force is otherwise justified under the Constitution, there is no constitutional duty to use non-deadly alternatives first." The court further noted that "[t]he Fourth

Amendment does not require officers to use the least intrusive or even less intrusive alternatives in search and seizure cases. The only test is whether what the police officers actually did was reasonable." The Court further noted that "we recognize that the decision to shoot can only be made after the briefest reflection, so brief that 'reflection' is the wrong word."

27. TASER is actually an acronym of "Thomas A. Swift Electric Rifle," a reference to a fictional science fiction character from the 1930s. The devices were actually developed in the 1970s by Jack Cover.

28. Nick Lewer and Neil Davison of the Bradford Non-Lethal Weapons Research Project (http://www.bradford.ac.uk/acad/nlw/research_reports/docs/BNLWRP_Janes_Oct05.pdf) refer to this problem as "mission creep from 'alternative to lethal force' to 'indiscriminate compliance tool.'"

29. For additional information on Taser deployment and safety, see Clark Kimerer, Chief of Staff and Chair et al. *A Less Lethal Options Program for Seattle Police Department: A Report with Recommendations*. 2000. Available online at http://www.cityofseattle.net/police/Publications/forg/forg_report.pdf.

30. Federal law enforcement has done a more comprehensive job of instituting guidelines and training for Taser use by its officers. State agencies continue to lag behind. See GOA report GAO-05-464, 2005. "Taser Weapons: Use of Tasers by Selected Law Enforcement Agencies."

31. Charlie Mesloh et al. in the report mentioned in note no. 28 report that the largest reason for Taser ineffectiveness is that the officer deploying the Taser missed the subject and 38% of the Taser deployments in that study were ineffective for that reason. Though increased training will not ensure 0% misses, it should certainly increase the overall effectiveness. When we take into account the overall effectiveness data above, it seems clear that the Taser, while of great value, should not be viewed as a "magic bullet" in every situation.

32. For an overview of the developing national standards, see U.S. Department of Justice, Office of Community Oriented Policing, 2006. *Conducted Energy Devices: Development of Standards for Consistency and Guidance.*

33. OC gas is also deployable as a "pepperball" projectile that can be fired from one of several devices. The use of the pepperball projectile is much more limited that the aerosol form of the gas.

34. As a cautionary note, where reported deaths have been linked to the use of OC spray by law enforcement, an overwhelming majority of them has been linked to the presence of drug use by the subject or a combination of drug use and other factors such as disease. See Charles Petty. 2004. *Deaths in Police Confrontations When Oleoresin Capsicum Is Used (A Study of 63 Incidents).* Available online at http://www.ncjrs.gov/pdffiles1/nij/grants/204029.pdf.

35. U.S. Department of Justice, National Institute of Justice. 1994. *Oleoresin Capsicum: Pepper Spray as a Force Alternative* Available online at http://www.ncjrs.gov/pdffiles1/nij/grants/181655.pdf Michael Bowling and Monica Gaines. 2000.

Evaluation of Oleoresin Capsicum (OC) Use by Law Enforcement Agencies: Impact on Injuries to Officers and Suspects, Summary of Research Findings. Available online at http://www.ncjrs.gov/pdffiles1/nij/grants/184935.pdf.

36. Memorandum of Agreement between the United States Department of Justice and the City of Cincinnati, Ohio and the Cincinnati Police Department, April 12, 2002. Available online at http://www.cincinnati-oh.gov/police/downloads/police_pdf5112.pdf.

37. See T. Cox et al. 1987. "Blunt Force Head Trauma from Police Impact Weapons: Some Skeletal and Neuropsychological Considerations," *Journal of Police Science and Administration* 15: 56–62.

38. See T. Cox et al. 1985. "Police Use of Metal Flashlights as Weapons: An Analysis of Relevant Problems," *Journal of Police Science and Management* 13(3): 244–249.

39. For a related discussion, see Bruce Siddle. 1999. *The Impact of the Sympathetic Nervous System on Use of Force Investigations.* Milstadt, IL: PPCT Management Systems.

40. Operation Order
    Situation
        Enemy
        Friendly
        Attach/detachments
    Mission
    Execution
        Concept of operation
                Maneuver
                Fire Support
        Obstacles
        Subunits mission
        Coordinating instructions
    Service Support
    (from infantry leaders' reference card GTA 7-1-31 June 1987, distribution: U.S. Army Training and Audiovisual Support Centers (TASCs). Approved for public release; distribution unlimited).

41. Concept of operation (plan "B" contingency plan) (Commanders and senior staff should have a contingency plan held in reserve when possible and it should only be disseminated to all units and individuals when the commander decides to implement the contingency plan; to do otherwise could confuse the other officers.)

42. See also Ruby-Ridge Weaver Hearings, September 6, 1995, Cnn.com, "FBI Shooters Defend Ruby Ridge Actions," September 15, 1995, Cnn.com.

43. Opening Statement of Louis J. Freeh, Director Federal Bureau of Investigation Before the Subcommittee on Terrorism, Technology, and Government Information Committee on the Judiciary United States Senate, Washington, DC, Ruby Ridge Hearing, October 19, 1995.

44. See the Opening Statement of Louis J. Freeh, Director Federal Bureau of Investigation Before the Subcommittee on Terrorism, Technology, and Government Information Committee on the Judiciary United States Senate, Washington, DC, Ruby Ridge Hearing, October 19, 1995.

45. "SWAT Team Members: FBI Shooter Rules 'Crazy' at Ruby Ridge," www. Cnn.com/US/9510/ruby_ridge/, October 14, 1995.

46. The siege by law enforcement in Waco, Texas, also had tragic consequences and provides some lessons not dissimilar to those from the siege at Ruby Ridge. For an exceptional account of the siege at Waco, see Stuart A. Wright, ed. 1995. *Armageddon in Waco: Critical Perspectives on the Branch Davidian Conflict.* Chicago: University of Chicago Press.

47. "Death of a Red Sox Fan Leads to Stricter Rules," Pam Belluck and Katie Zezima, *New York Times,* October 23, 2004.

48. See also "Student's Death Returns Crowd Control to the Fore," Fox Butterfield, *New York Times,* November 1, 2004.

3. Custodial Interrogation

1. *Florida v. Bostick,* 501 US 429 (1991).

2. *Florida v. Bostick,* 501 US 429 (1991); See also *California v. Beheler,* 463 US 1121 (1983) in which the Court declares that Miranda safeguards become applicable as soon as a suspect's freedom of action is curtailed to a degree associated with formal arrest.

3. *Florida v. Bostick,* 501 US 429 (1991); see also *United States v. Drayton,* 536 US 194 (2002) upholding the ruling in Bostick on similar facts; also see *California v. Hodari D.,* 499 US 621 (1991) holding that a seizure does not occur so long as a reasonable person would feel free to disregard the police and go about his business.

4. *Miranda v. Arizona* (consolidated with *Westover v. United States, Vignera v. New York,* and *California v. Stewart*), 384 US 436 (1966).

5. See "Intelligence Truth Extraction: A Classic Text on Interrogating Enemy Captives Offers a Counterintuitive Lesson on the Best Way to Get Information," Stephen Budiansky, *The Atlantic,* June 2005.

6. Fifth Amendment, United States Constitution, Sixth Amendment United States Constitution.

7. *Miranda v. Arizona,* 384 US 436 (1966).

8. *Miranda v. Arizona,* 384 US 436 (1966).

9. *Miranda v. Arizona,* 384 US 436 (1966). Emphasis added. This rule was upheld by the Supreme Court in *Dickerson v. United States,* 120 S.Ct. 2326 (2000).

10. *Dickerson v. United States.* 120 S.Ct. 2326 (2000).

11. For a complete review of the results of the Dickerson decision on law enforcement, please see Charles Weisselberg. 2001. "In the Stationhouse after Dickerson," *Michigan Law Review* 99(5): 1121–1163.

12. *Miranda v. Arizona*, 384 US 436 (1966).

13. As an additional protection for both suspects and the officers who interrogate them, some jurisdictions have mandated that all custodial interrogations be contemporaneously recorded. While there was initial resistance to the mandate, the process has proven to be ultimately beneficial to law enforcement officers in the performance of their duties. See Thomas Sullivan. 2004. "Police Experience with Recording Custodial Interrogations," *Judicature* 88(3): 132–136.

14. "The Conscience of the Colonel," *The Wall Street Journal*, A1, Saturday/Sunday March 31–April 1, 2007.

15. For a fascinating and detailed article regarding custodial interrogation crossing the line into torture, see "The Conscience of the Colonel," *The Wall Street Journal*, A1, Saturday/Sunday March 31–April 1, 2007.

16. See "Tortured Logic" Anthony Lagouranis, *New York Times*, A 25, Tuesday February 28, 2006.

17. *Ashcraft v. Tennessee*, 322 US 143 (1944).

18. *Ashcraft v. Tennessee*, 322 US 143 (1944).

19. An exculpatory statement is one in which the person speaking says that he did not do it or that he was not involved. An inculpatory statement is one in which the person speaking says that he did do it or that he was involved. Either type of statement can be incriminating.

20. *Watts v. Indiana*, 338 US 49 (1949).

21. *Watts v. Indiana*, 338 US 49 (1949).

22. *Rhode Island v. Innis*, 446 US 291 (1980).

23. *Rhode Island v. Innis*, 446 US 291 (1980).

24. *Rhode Island v. Innis*, 446 US 291 (1980).

25. *Rhode Island v. Innis*, 446 US 291 (1980).

26. See *New York v. Quarles*, 467 US 649 (1984) public safety exception to Miranda warnings, and *Illinois v. Perkins*, 496 US 292 (1990), holding Miranda warnings not required when suspect is unaware he is speaking to law enforcement officer and gives voluntary statement; *Berkemer v. McCarty*, 468 US 420 (1984), traffic stop more analogous to Terry Stop and Miranda warnings not required for ordinary traffic stop. For further discussion of these cases and the limitations on Miranda, see Kate Greenwood. 1998. "Custodial Interrogations," *Georgetown Law Journal* 86(5): 1318–1338.

27. *Garrity v. New Jersey*, 385 US 493 (1967).

28. *Knowles v. Iowa*, 525 US 113 (1998), quoting *United States v. Robinson*, 414 US 218 (1973); *Michigan v. Long*, 463 US 1032 (1983) extends principles of a Terry Stop to traffic stops.

29. See *Atwater v. Largo Vista*, 532 US 318 (2001).
30. *Katz v. United States*, 389 US 347 (1967).
31. *Whren v United States*, 517 US 806 (1996).
32. *Whren v. United States*, 517 US 806 (1996).
33. *Whren v. United States*, 517 US 806 (1996).
34. *Atwater v. City of Largo Vista*, 532 US 318 (2001).

4. Liability of Law Enforcement Officers

1. See also "immunity" and "qualified immunity," *Black's Law Dictionary*. 752–753.
2. Most people agree that the total number of civil suit filings against law enforcement officers has increased enormously. The total numbers are difficult to ascertain but it is estimated that there are about 30,000 lawsuits filed annually. That number is up from 1,741 in 1967, to 3,894 in 1971, 13,500 in 1976, and approximately 25,000 by 1982. The trend is for more actions to be brought in the future. (Cited in Howard Rahtz. 2003. *Understanding Police Use of Force*. Monsey, NY: Criminal Justice Press, p.110. For the evolution of standards of liability, see also Darrell Ross. 2001. "An Assessment of *Graham v. Connor* Ten Years Later" available at http://www.emeraldinsight.com/1363-951X.htm.
3. U.S. Code, Title 42, Section 1983 (2004).
4. For an excellent and very complete discussion of civil liability of police, see Victor E. Kappeler. 2006. *Critical Issues in Police Civil Liability*, 4th edition. Long Grove, IL: Waveland Press, Inc.
5. DeWolf and Allen. *Tort Law and Practice* 16:353, Washington Practice Series, citing *Robinson v. City of Seattle*, 119 Wash.2d. 34 (1992).
6. *Canton v. Harris*, 489 US 378 (1989).
7. *Canton v. Harris*, 489 US 378 (1989).
8. *Canton v. Harris*, 489 US 378 (1989), citing *Springfield v. Kibbe*, 480 US 257 (1987).
9. *Canton v. Harris*, 489 US 378 (1989).
10. *Graham v. Connor*, 490 US 386(1989).
11. *Graham v. Connor*, 490 US 386 (1989).
12. *Graham v. Connor*, 490 US 386(1989). Emphasis added.
13. *Wilson v. Garcia*, 471 US 261 (1985).
14. *Saucier v. Katz*, 533 US 194 (2001).
15. *Saucier v. Katz*, 533 US 194 (2001). Emphasis added.
16. *Saucier v. Katz*, 533 US 194 (2001). Emphasis added.
17. *Saucier v. Katz*, 533 US 194 (2001). Emphasis added.
18. *Saucier v. Katz*, 533 US 194 (2001).
19. *Brosseau v. Haugen* 543 US 194 (2004).
20. *Brosseau v. Haugen* 543 US 194 (2004). Emphasis added.

21. *Brosseau v. Haugen* 543 US 194 (2004).
22. "To Serve and Protect, but Politely, With Complaints of Rudeness Rising, New York Police Cadets Receive New Training," Thomas J. Lueck, *New York Times,* July 29, 2007.
23. "Seattle Police Go after One of Their Own: 'He Tarnished His Badge,' Kerlikowske Says of Heroin Suspect," Ian Ith, Seattle Times.com, September 29, 2002.
24. "Dallas Police Officer Fired after Indictments in Fake Drug Case," CNN.com, April 29, 2003.
25. "Agent Indicted after Hearing to Review '99 Drug Sting," Simon Romero, *New York Times,* April 25, 2003.
26. "4 Miami Police Officers Convicted of Conspiracy in Shootings," Dana Canedy, *New York Times,* April 10, 2003.
27. "2 Ex-Detectives Guilty in Killings,"Alan Feuer, *New York Times,* April 7, 2006.
28. "Officials Investigate Broad Corruption in Atlanta Police Dept.," Shaila Dewan and Brenda Goodman, *New York Times,* April 27, 2007.
29. "Officer Charged in Shooting," Bill Morlin and Christopher Rodkey, *Spokesman-Review,* April 17, 2007.
30. Howard Rahtz. 2003. *Understanding Police Use of Force.* Monsey, NY: Criminal Justice Press.
31. See Mary Cheh. 1996, *Police Violence: Understanding and Controlling Police Abuse of Force.* William A. Geller, Hans Toch, eds. New Haven, CT: Yale University Press.
32. See http://www.pbs.org/wgbh/pages/frontline/shows/lapd/scandal/.
33. See http://www.usdoj.gov/crt/split/documents/lapdnoti.htm. The Department of Justice brought this action against the LAPD et al. pursuant to United States Code title 42 Section 14141.
34. See the Consent Decree, *United States of America v. City of Los Angeles et al.* in the United States District Court for the Central District of California, 2000.
35. "Police Ombudsman Proposed," Karen Dorn Steele, *Spokesman-Review,* p. B-1, April 14, 2007.
36. U.S. Code, Title 42, Section 14141 (2004). Sections 1985, 1986, and 1987, among others, of the U.S. Code, Title 42 (2004) also provide legal avenues and remedies. This book is not exhaustive in its exploration of legal theories and remedies available in police abuse of force cases, but it does focus on the most common and arguably the most useful.
37. "Outside Monitor to Oversee Detroit Police," Eric Slater, LA Times.com, June 13, 2003. See also the press release from the Department of Justice titled "Justice Department Files Consent Decrees Concluding Investigation of Detroit Police Department". www.usdoj.gov/opa/pr/2003/June/03_crt_352.htm.
38. "Federal Monitor to Oversee Detroit Police," Sarah Freeman, Associated Press Writer, *Findlay Legal News and Commentary,* June 12, 2003.

5. High-Speed Pursuit

1. *Scott v. Harris* (no. 05–1631), argued February 26, 2007 and decided April 30, 2007.
2. Please see Chapter 2 for a discussion of *Garner v. Tennessee.*
3. See *Saucier v. Katz* 533 US 194 (2001).
4. The Court of Appeals had written that the suspect had maintained control of his car, slowed down for intersections, used his signal to indicate turns, and therefore posed no serious danger to anyone out on the road. As Justice Scalia wrote, "Indeed, reading the lower court's opinion, one gets the impression that [the suspect], rather than fleeing from police, was attempting to pass his driving test." In overturning the lower court, Justice Scalia suggested a far different interpretation of the events on the video, "Far from being the cautious and controlled driver the lower court depicts, what we see on the video more closely resembles a Hollywood-style car chase of the most frightening sort placing police officers and innocent bystanders alike at great risk of injury" (see *Scott v. Harris*).
5. *Scott v. Harris* (no. 05–1631), argued February 26, 2007 and decided April 30, 2007.
6. In 2004, for instance, California alone had had 7,321 police pursuit reports by law enforcement (see, Data Summary Report 2004. Sacramento, CA: California Highway Patrol, Office of Public Affairs, Pursuit Reporting System). While some similar reporting systems exist in some other states, it is difficult and problematic to generalize about the numbers nationally. However, the total numbers of pursuits is certainly considerable.
7. Most commonly, pursuits last less than five minutes; many occur at less than 40 miles per hour, and most crashes occur within the first two minutes of a pursuit (see Geoffrey P. Alpert, Dennis Jay Kenney, Roger G. Dunham, and William C. Smith. 2000. *Police Pursuits: What We Know*. Police Executive Research Forum, Washington, DC).
8. From Hugh Nugent et al. 1990. *Restrictive Policies for High-Speed Police Pursuits*. National Institute of Justice.
9. The definition offered by Nugent et al. is not the only definition that is used. The definition used by the International Association of Chiefs of Police, for instance, contains many of the same elements but is slightly different. That organization defines a police pursuit as, "an active attempt by an officer in an authorized emergency vehicle to apprehend a fleeing suspect who is actively attempting to elude the police" (see "Vehicular Pursuit, Model Policy," 1996. IACP National Law Enforcement Policy Center: Alexandria, VA). Different definitions, while similar, may yield very different results. Consider this definition of pursuit from Geoffrey Alpert and Patrick Anderson. 1986. *"The Most Deadly Force: Police Pursuits," Justice Quarterly* 3(1): 4 as "an active attempt by a law enforcement officer operating an emergency vehicle to apprehend alleged criminals in a moving motor vehicle, when

the driver of the vehicle, in an attempt to avoid apprehension, *significantly increases his or her speed* or takes other evasive action" (emphasis added) and it becomes clear that definitions in these cases matters a lot.

10. The numbers can vary wildly. Some reports put the number of annual pursuit-related deaths at only about 350 while other suggest numbers as high as 2500 with as many as an additional 55,000 injured. Probably both the high and low numbers are incorrect (see John Hill. 2002. "High Speed Police Pursuits: Dangers, Dynamics, and Risk Reduction," *FBI Law Enforcement Bulletin,* July).

11. This database was created in 1982 to track police pursuit crashes and fatalities. The limitations of the data are evident. There is no comprehensive data on total pursuits across the United States; the reporting requirements vary between states and, most importantly, fatalities that occur outside of the specific definition of "pursuit" employed are not reportable to the system. This is especially important for pursuits that continue once the occupants of the pursued vehicle have left the vehicle (once the vehicle pursuit has ended) or once the pursuing officer has discontinued the active pursuit. As reported by H. Range Huston et al., significant number of individuals leave their vehicle and flee on foot at some point, terminating the vehicle pursuit. As many as 178 fatalities occurred between 1998 and 2004 in California alone in these types of cases but, because they were outside of the definition of vehicle pursuit, could not be reported to the database (see H. Range Hutson, Phillip L. Rice Jr., Jasroop K. Chana, Demetrios N. Kyriacou, Yuchiao Chang, and Robert M. Miller. 2007. "A Review of Police Pursuit Fatalities in the United States from 1982–2004," *Prehospital Emergency Care* 11(3) (July–Sept.): 278–283).

12. F. P. Rivara and C. D. Mack 2004. "Motor Vehicle Crash Deaths Related to Police Pursuits in the United States" *Injury Prevention* 10(2): 93–95.

13. These data are certainly incomplete although to what extent is unclear. The lack of mandatory reporting requirements and consistent definitions may result in these numbers being as little as one half of the actual incidents per year (see D. P. Van Blaricom. 1998. "He Flees To Pursue or Not to Pursue: That is the Question," *Police* 22(11).

14. H. Range Hutson, Phillip L. Rice Jr., Jasroop K. Chana, Demetrios N. Kyriacou, Yuchiao Chang, and Robert M. Miller. 2007. "A Review of Police Pursuit Fatalities in the United States from 1982–2004," *Prehospital Emergency Care,* 11(3) (July–Sept.): 278–283.

15. The authors make special note of the disturbing fact that 25% of the officer fatalities resulting from police pursuits involved alcohol intoxication on the part of the officer killed. "How often this occurs during pursuits is unknown, and it requires additional study and prevention strategies." H. Range Hutson, Phillip L. Rice Jr., Jasroop K. Chana, Demetrios N. Kyriacou, Yuchiao Chang, and Robert M. Miller. 2007. "A Review of Police Pursuit Fatalities in the United States from 1982–2004," *Prehospital Emergency Care* 11(3) (July–Sept.): 278–283.

16. There are additionally some important lower court cases that deal with questions of pursuit and pursuit policy. See Dominick Pape. 2001. "Police Pursuits and Civil Liability," *FBI Law Enforcement Bulletin* (July): 16–21, for a discussion of several of these lower court decisions as they relate to civil liability.

17. *California v. Hodari*. 111 S.Ct. 1547 (1991).

18. For an interesting discussion of this case and its implications for the Fourth Amendment and Exclusionary Rule, see Timothy Devetski. 1992. "Fourth Amendment Protection against Unreasonable Seizure of the Person: The New (?) Common Law Arrest Test for Seizure," *The Journal of Law and Criminology* 82(4): 747–772.

19. *Brower v. County of Inyo* 489 US 593 (1989).

20. *Brower v. County of Inyo* 489 US 593 (1989).

21. *Brower v. County of Inyo* 489 US 593 (1989).

22. *Brower v. County of Inyo* 489 US 593 (1989).

23. *Brower v. County of Inyo* 489 US 593 (1989).

24. *City of Canton v. Harris* 489 US 378 (1989).

25. *City of Canton v. Harris* 489 US 378 (1989).

26. *City of Canton v. Harris* 489 US 378 (1989).

27. In *City of Canton*, the Court differentiated between unsatisfactory training, insufficient training, or even officer error and "deliberate indifference." The Court explained, "[i]n resolving the issue of a city's liability, the focus must be on adequacy of the training program in relation to the tasks the particular officers must perform. That a particular officer may be unsatisfactorily trained will not alone suffice to fasten liability on the city, for the officer's shortcomings may have resulted from factors other than a faulty training program. It may be, for example, that an otherwise sound program has occasionally been negligently administered. Neither will it suffice to prove that an injury or accident could have been avoided if an officer had had better or more training, sufficient to equip him to avoid the particular injury-causing conduct. Such a claim could be made about almost any encounter resulting in injury, yet not condemn the adequacy of the program to enable officers to respond properly to the usual and recurring situations with which they must deal. And plainly, adequately trained officers occasionally make mistakes; the fact that they do says little about the training program or the legal basis for holding the city liable." This creates a difficult standard indeed for any plaintiff but that should not encourage laxness in policymaking or in training.

28. D. P. Van Blaricom. 2004. "Control of Police Vehicular Pursuit," *Law Enforcement Executive Forum* (January): 2.

29. Geoffrey Alpert. 1997. "Police Pursuit: Policy and Training," *Research in Brief*. National Institute of Justice, U.S. Department of Justice, May 1997.

30. D. P. Van Blaricom. 2004. "Control of Police Vehicular Pursuit," *Law Enforcement Executive Forum* (January): 2.

31. Not everyone believes that such a balancing is being accomplished with current policies. Travis Jensen argues in "Cooling the Hot Pursuit" (73 Ind. L. J. 1277, 1282–90 [1998]) argues that what is needed is a categorical approach that clearly distinguishes different types of offenders and allows pursuit only for some types, regardless of other circumstances.

32. D. P. Van Blaricom. 2004. "Control of Police Vehicular Pursuit," *Law Enforcement Executive Forum* (January): 1. The sample policy referenced in the quotation is the 1996 International Association of Chiefs of Police (IACP) sample vehicular pursuit policy, and can be found online at http://www.pursuitwatch.org/pursuit_policies/IACP%20Model%20Policy.pdf.

33. Hugh Nugent et al. 1990. *Restrictive Policies for High-Speed Police Pursuits*. National Institute of Justice.

34. See John Hill. 2002. "High-speed Police Pursuits: Dangers, Dynamics, and Risk Reduction," *FBI Law Enforcement Bulletin*, July.

35. Some jurisdictions have attempted to create specific use of force continua solely for pursuit as a use of force. These "pursuit Management" continua are often very complex and require not only additional training but incredible decision control on the part of the officer to execute. As with all use of force continua, they are beneficial only if they are accessible to officers through training and if they are not so overly complex that they cannot be utilized in very short timeframe decision making processes. A sample of a pursuit policy continuum can be reviewed online at http://www.sashley.com/articles/motorvehiclepursuit.htm.

36. Auto Arrestors are devices that emit a high energy pulse that shorts out the electrical system of a passing vehicle rendering the vehicle inoperative.

Conclusion:
Reasonable Use of Force by Police

1. Randall Kennedy, ed. 1997. *Race, Crime, and the Law*. New York: Pantheon Books.

2. Jerome Skolnick and James Fyfe. 1994. *Above the Law: Police and the Excessive Use of Force*. New York: Free Press.

3. See Brian Arnspiger and Gordon A Bowers. 1996. "Integrated Use-of-Force Training Program—Focus on Training," *The FBI Law Enforcement Bulletin*, November.

4. Howard Rahtz. 2002. *Community Policing: A Handbook for Beat Cops and Supervisors*. Monsey, NY: Criminal Justice Press.

5. Robert Trojanowicz. 1989. Preventing Civil Disturbances: A Community Policing Approach. Paper. National Center for Community Policing: Michigan State University. (Available at http://www1.cj.msu.edu/~people/cp/pcd.html)